Michael

Roy Williams addresses his team in the moments before the Tar Heels take the floor in the national championship game against Illinois.

"Last year we had a reunion," he says, referencing the Lettermen's Reunion that drew hundreds of Tar Heel basketball alums back to Chapel Hill. "Four of the five starters from the 1957 championship team were at that reunion. . . . They're always remembered as a national championship team. And 47 or 48 years later, the relationships they have and the memories they have are some of the strongest things about them.

"You guys have a chance to have that same feeling. You guys can get this done tonight. Somebody has to win. Why not let it be us?"

The message is powerful, but Williams debated using it.

"I fought with myself about whether to bring it up," he says. "But I thought it was a way for them to be led by their dreams, not pushed by their problems."

Led by Their Dreams

The Inside Story of Carolina's Journey to the 2005 National Championship

Adam Lucas

Steve Kirschner

Matt Bowers

THE LYONS PRESS
Guilford, Connecticut
An imprint of The Globe Pequot Press

The Lyons Press is an imprint of The Globe Pequot Press

2   4   6   8   10   9   7   5   3   1

Printed in the United States of America

Book design: Casey Shain
Project editor: Sarah Mazer
Title page photograph by Patrick Schneider/Charlotte Observer

ISBN 1-59228-918-5

Library of Congress Cataloging-in-Publication Data is available on file.

Contents

The Warm-Up

Acknowledgments .... *vii*

Foreword by Dean Smith .... *ix*

Preface .... *xi*

The Action

Chapter 1: **See the Future** *1*

Chapter 2: **Workdays in Maui** *5*

Chapter 3: **The Silence & the Roar** *13*

Chapter 4: **Building a Program** *19*

Chapter 5: **The Difference of Defense** *25*

Chapter 6: **The Blue Team** *31*

Chapter 7: **History Repeats Itself** *37*

Chapter 8: **Awards & Rewards** *41*

Chapter 9: **The Perils of Hesitation** *47*

Chapter 10: **Back on Track** *51*

Chapter 11: **Road Warriors** *57*

Chapter 12: **Senior Day** *65*

Chapter 13: **Letdown in D.C.** *75*

Chapter 14: **The Spark Returns** *79*

Chapter 15: **Two Steps to St. Louis** *85*

Chapter 16: **The Pit** *95*

Chapter 17: **National Champions** *105*

Chapter 18: **Saying Goodbye** *117*

The Highlights

In Their Own Words: Coaches

Roy Williams 123

Jerod Haase 141

Joe Holladay 145

C. B. McGrath 149

Steve Robinson 153

In Their Own Words: Players

Raymond Felton 157

Jackie Manuel 167

Sean May 177

Rashad McCants 185

David Noel 193

Melvin Scott 201

Jawad Williams 209

Marvin Williams 217

The Wrap-Up

A Tribute to Burgess McSwain 225

2004–05 Team Roster 229

2004–05 Season Record 230

Postseason Notes 233

Awards and Honors 236

Acknowledgments

In January 2005, a few days after Carolina dismantled Maryland, scoring 109 points in the process, *Tar Heel Monthly* publisher and TarHeelBlue.com contributing writer Adam Lucas popped his head into my office at the Smith Center and uttered the unthinkable.

"This team is going to win the national championship and when it does, we need to publish a book," he said.

I responded, "I've been thinking the same thing since the flight home from Maui. I've always wanted to work on a book after Carolina wins a national championship."

Then, not willing to invoke the time-honored jinx of talking about a championship before actually winning one, we didn't utter another word about a book for months.

Four months, in fact—until April 4, when less than five minutes after Carolina won the 2005 NCAA title, my cell phone rang. I didn't know it at the time because I was on the court trying to round up Roy Williams, Sean May, and others for interviews, but the call came from Adam.

"Congratulations. See you in the interview room. We start the book tonight."

Matt Bowers and I thought that Carolina fans would forever enjoy three things as they look back on the championship: great photos, Adam's insight on the season, and first-person accounts from the players and coaches who lived out their basketball dreams. So that is what we give you in the ensuing pages.

This book is dedicated to the student-athletes, coaches, managers, and staff that made it such a delightfully memorable Carolina basketball season. Those of us who were fortunate enough to be along for the ride thank you.

Thanks to the players and coaches for sitting down with us after the season and sharing their memories, both for the DVD (*Team Carolina*) and *Led by*

Their Dreams. It was almost as much fun listening to you talk about the season as it was watching it happen in the first place.

Thanks to Coach Williams for the two-and-a-half-hour interview he gave us and for allowing us to include motivational statements from the team's practice plans—the "Thought for the Day"—throughout the book. It's interesting to see which statements foretold something that was about to happen and which ones were teaching points to correct misguided habits.

Thanks to Carolina Athletics director of photography Jeffrey Camarati, who spent countless hours preparing the photos (many of which he also shot)

for this book. Thanks also to the talented photographers and photo agencies whose artistic view of the season you hold in your hands. They include Jim Bounds; Bob Donnan; J. D. Lyon Jr.; Peyton Williams; Jim Hawkins; Robert Crawford; Andrew Wilcox; Kevin Cox at Wire Image; Dan Sears; Porter Binks and Sheryl Spain at *Sports Illustrated;* Bob Leverone at the *Sporting News;* and Getty Images.

Thanks to Ken Cleary, who manned the camera for roughly 15 hours of video interviews, and to Athletic Communications staff members, who patiently transcribed the interviews (Sean Alford, Loreal Andrews, Danielle Appelman, Brent Bearden, Kim Conrad, Noelle Dean, Whitney Freeman, Jeff McLerran, Ashley Miller, Lauren Brownlow, Terry Roberts, and Liz Ryan). And to Lee Snyder for proofreading the first-person accounts.

Thanks to Director of Athletics Dick Baddour; Athletics Marketing Director Norwood Teague; and Tom McCarthy, Casey Shain, and Sarah Mazer at Lyons Press for their assistance and encouragement.

Most important, thanks to our families—Crystal and Sam Bowers; Jeanne, Ryan, and Emilie Kirschner; and Stephanie, McKay, and Asher Lucas—for putting up with more of our absences after the Final Four. We hope that someday our kids will be able to experience their own pursuit of a national championship. Regardless, you are our ultimate prize!

—STEVE KIRSCHNER

Foreword

When I watched Carolina play in the Final Four

in St. Louis, I was mostly a cheerleader. In the years since my retirement from coaching, I've discovered what it is like to be a fan—it's nerve-wracking.

Coach Williams invited Coach Guthridge and me to go with the team to the Maui Invitational at the start of the season. I was very nervous watching the games. I found that I would write things down, as if I was scouting the team. Coach Williams knows what is going on, and I didn't even want to give him my notes—but putting my thoughts on paper did help me be less nervous.

Of course I was a little tense in St. Louis. On Saturday night I sat in the stands, but on Monday night I moved into a box with a former player,

Michael Jordan. It would be difficult for Michael to go into coaching because he is very demanding. While we were watching the game, he'd say things like, "Why did they do that?" or "What were they thinking there?" I finally had to tell him the players on the floor couldn't hear him.

But the players did hear Roy Williams. And on the very first day of practice, Coach let them know that defense was going to be a number-one priority in a striking way: by taking the rims off the baskets. That was one of Coach Williams's innovations, and it was an excellent idea.

The championship team had very good senior leaders, and they had seen the year before how close they were to being a great team. Everyone came back in game shape, ready to work, and their collective effort was remarkable. Defensively, they tried very hard, and that's something that can't be coached. Offensively, they played unselfishly from day one. Shot selection had been a problem at times last year, but it was enjoyable to watch this team move the ball and work to get a better shot.

From the beginning of the 2004–05 season, it was apparent that the Tar Heels would be a national contender. But in college basketball you can never say for certain that a specific team is a national championship team. In a best-of-seven series, it's possible to have a favorite. But in a single-elimination format like the NCAA Tournament, anything can happen.

Coach Williams knew that this team was capable of playing at a very high level. It was a matter of getting better every day, of committing to improvements in every aspect of the game. The players made that commitment, and in the process the team took Carolina fans everywhere on a great journey. I was lucky to be among those fans, along for the ride.

Dean Smith

Preface

Americans love to label people and things to more
easily identify them. One day we woke to a nation of red states and blue states.
People are Coke or Pepsi, Red Sox or Yankees, Gordon or Little E, Duke or
Carolina.

One April Monday evening in St. Louis, it came
down to Team versus Talent. It was easy for the so-
called experts to boil the national championship
down to those two words. Illinois, with its lone loss
and unselfish play, was the embodiment of team ball;
Carolina, the experts said, was a talented yet dysfunc-
tional group of future lottery picks.

How did it come to that? The Tar Heels had
already won 32 games, claimed the ACC regular-
season title by taking six of eight road games in the
best conference in the country, and led the nation in
scoring and assists. So why were we inundated with
talking heads and newspaper ink spouting that the
impetuous Tar Heels were 40 minutes of Orange from
imploding under the famous Arch?

Labels, that's how. Carolina's script for the season read this way: Future Hall of Fame coach enters

year two, leading a program riddled with gifted but selfish athletes. He butts heads
with the leading scorer; is exasperated by the decisions of a sometimes bedazzling,
sometimes out-of-control point guard; and yet has the most talented starting five
in the country and a freshman phenom to boot as the number-one man off the
bench.

Even UNC followers quietly questioned the team's determination and heart.
When you think of Carolina's 1993 national champions, you remember George
Lynch's leadership and resolve, Eric Montross's rugged inside play, Derrick
Phelps's in-your-face pressure defense, and overall unselfish team ball. You think
of the 21-point comeback against Florida State and the erasure of double-figure
deficits to Arkansas, Cincinnati, and Michigan. It wasn't a lineup loaded with
future NBA stars, but it was a great team.

Fast-forward to 2005. Commentators said the Tar Heels were fun to watch—they lit up the scoreboard in December and January—but would fold like a cheap suitcase when March rolled in and teams tightened the screws and got them in a half-court game.

So much for labels. The one word that everyone forgot to mention was the one that most accurately depicted the 2004–05 Tar Heels: tough.

When the final, errant Illinois shot appropriately fell into Sean May's hands, the toughest bunch of kids in the country reigned as the best *team* in the land. It was a national championship forged through adversity and through trust. Would the players trust that teammates had their backs? Would they trust the legendary coach, whose mandate was to play on both ends of the floor and to play for the name on the front of the jersey, not the one on the back? And ultimately, would they trust themselves to sacrifice fleeting moments of individual glory for the team prize at the end of the journey? Almost all year the answer was a resounding *yes*.

Looking back, it should have been so obvious. Yes, there was talent; that is undeniable. But beyond that they had resiliency, maturity, pride, and toughness. There were numerous occasions, some before the championship year, when they could have packed it in and called it a day.

Seniors Jackie Manuel, Melvin Scott, and Jawad Williams were hardened by their experiences as freshmen (2001–02), when they were part of the worst season in school history. The roller-coaster events of the following year, if put to a Hollywood producer, might have been deemed too bizarre to be believed. Yet the players stayed. Even after the fall 2002 arrival of the Big Three—May, Raymond Felton, and Rashad McCants—there were losses too painful to erase from memory: a 40-point debacle in College Park; a 24-point lead blown in

Tallahassee; a coast-to-coast overtime drive by Duke's Chris Duhon; a final-play meltdown in Charlottesville.

Even in the glorious championship season, how many times were the Tar Heels on the precipice of cashing it in and reverting to old habits? They lost to unheralded Santa Clara; frittered away a double-digit lead at Florida State; turned the ball over 23 times and missed a final opportunity to win at Duke; were plagued by illness late in the ACC chase (losing the mercurial McCants and his 15 points a game for four games straight); trailed the Blue Devils by 9 points at the final television break on Senior Day; laid an egg in the ACC Tournament; and faced a 13-point deficit to a four-guard Villanova lineup that would neither miss nor back down.

At the Final Four, nothing came easy. The Tar Heels had to overcome a 5-point halftime deficit, the largest of the season in a victory, in the national semifinals against Michigan State, a physical squad that already had eliminated Duke and Kentucky. In the final act of this drama, they raced to a 15-point lead, then watched Illinois rain down three-pointers to even the game with five minutes to play.

But the Tar Heels' toughness won out. They made plays. All year Roy Williams told them how to win when everything was on the line: "Get must-stops." "Don't give in." "Find a way." So Felton buried a three, Marvelous Marvin tipped one in, Manuel and David Noel denied open looks, and Felton read a play perfectly to steal the ball, the game, and the crown.

Give me a group that could overcome all of that and go 33–4 and I'll give you the 2005 national champions. The best *team* in college basketball this year and one of the toughest Tar Heel teams in our rich history. That's a label worth printing.

11.05.04 Winston-Salem State (exh.)	12.21.04 Vermont	02.06.05 at Florida State
11.12.04 Mount Olive (exh.)	12.28.04 UNC Wilmington	02.09.05 at Duke
11.19.04 Santa Clara (Oakland, CA)	12.30.04 Cleveland State	02.13.05 at Connecticut
11.22.04 BYU (Maui)	01.02.05 William & Mary	02.16.05 Virginia
11.23.04 Stanford or Tennessee (Maui)	01.08.05 Maryland	02.19.05 Clemson
11.24.04 TBA (Maui)	01.12.05 Georgia Tech	02.22.05 at North Carolina State
11.28.04 USC	01.15.05 at Wake Forest	02.27.05 at Maryland
12.01.04 at Indiana	01.19.05 at Clemson	03.03.05 Florida State
12.04.04 Kentucky	01.22.05 Miami	03.06.05 Duke
12.12.04 Loyola-Chicago	01.29.05 at Virginia	03.10.05 ACC Tournament
12.19.04 at Virginia Tech	02.03.05 North Carolina State	

See the
Future

CHAPTER ONE

**In the calm of a fall Chapel Hill after-
noon, three old men are asked to look
into the future.**

They're not really old. But Jawad Williams, Jackie Manuel,
and Melvin Scott seem that way when they spend the better part
of an hour recounting their basketball careers at North Carolina.
They can do it with laughter now. The bad times don't seem
quite as bad; the tears don't seem quite as painful; the 8–20
year doesn't seem . . . well, that year still seems as bad as ever.

They have spent enough time recounting the past. Now
they are asked to look into the future, to peer six months
ahead and describe what they see. Each looks away, casts his
eyes onto the Smith Center court. It's empty now, but they can
visualize everything that has happened over the summer. They
see Raymond Felton zipping across the court. They see Rashad
McCants launching three-pointers
from every spot within 30 feet of the
basket. They see Sean May, but not
the old Sean May—the new one who
features muscle where cheeseburgers
used to be. They see David Noel
finally healthy after last season's hand

*Scott, J. Williams, and
Manuel with champi-
onship memorabilia from
years past (opposite);
Williams enters the
Smith Center (above) and
Noel dunks (right) at Late
Night with Roy Williams.*

1

injury. They see a remarkable freshman, Marvin Williams, who has shown an uncanny mix of power and finesse during fall pickup games.

They see what they too often were not during the 2003–04 season. They see a team.

They see something else, too.

"I see a championship," Jawad Williams says. "Winning it would be something to write a book about."

They all see it. They describe how they picture the final moments, how they each want to climb the ladder and snip a piece of championship net. When they talk about it, they don't say, "I would . . ." They say, "I will . . ." It's not something that could happen. It's something that *will* happen.

"I will be going nuts up there," Scott says.

"I will be acting crazy," Manuel says.

"I will be myself," Williams says. "I'll be more laid-back than these guys."

Jawad Williams sits in front of his locker at Oakland Arena, eyes forward, back to the room.

He is not speaking. There isn't much to say. Santa Clara 77, North Carolina 66. That's Santa "just lost by 34 points to New Mexico last week" Clara 77, North "on the cover of *Sports Illustrated* as the preseason No. 1" Carolina 66.

Tar Heel players had spent much of the preseason talking about their commitment to doing the little things that had been absent during the 2003–04 season. Better defense. More sharing of the basketball. Better communication.

Defense? Carolina's scouting report on Santa Clara's Travis Niesen was simple: He likes to go over his right shoulder. Twenty-six points later, almost all of them over his right shoulder, the Tar Heels still haven't stopped him. Carolina coaches turn to each other on the bench, asking, "Why did we have a walk-through and a scouting report if they're not going to pay attention?"

Sharing the basketball? The Heels hand out 19 assists on 23 field goals, but just 3 of them come from point guard Quentin Thomas, who gets the start in his hometown in place of Raymond Felton, who is serving an NCAA-mandated one-game suspension. Teammates and coaches notice Thomas talk-

thought for the day

"It's amazing how much can be accomplished when no one cares who gets the credit."

—October 16, 2004

M. Williams displays his athleticism in a preseason game vs. Mount Olive (opposite); May at preseason media day (left).

JEFFREY A. CAMARATI

ing more than usual in the locker room before the game, a sign of nervousness. It shows on the floor; he also commits 3 turnovers.

Togetherness? "We had a little bit of that selfishness out there," Sean May says.

A little bit? The Tar Heels who skulk back to the team bus are virtually indistinguishable from last season's disappointing bunch. All the talk about a recommitment to defense (the Broncos make 59.1 percent of their second-half field goals) seems very hollow as the bus makes its way, quietly, back to the hotel.

"It's about as mad as I've ever been in coaching," Roy Williams says.

"That little attitude we had about how we were number one or we were this or we were that, it was all out the window after that game," Jackie Manuel says. "We came in too cocky."

The recovery process begins immediately. Noticing some teammates moping in the Tar Heel locker room, a handful of players, including Sean May and David Noel, stand up.

"Hey, nobody said we were going to go 36–0," May says. "Nobody said we were going to have a perfect season. It's just one game."

Immediate reaction to the game is mixed. Some players are more concerned than May, feeling too many similarities to last season. Some believe it is merely a hiccup. Assistant coach Joe Holladay, one of the fiercest competitors on the team, is philosophical. He knows that the Tar Heels are very different without Felton, the point guard who Roy Williams will later call "the closest player to indispensable I've ever coached."

The Heels can't lose Felton. With him, they can bounce back. Without him, they are paralyzed.

Workdays in Maui

CHAPTER TWO

Roy Williams is figuring out how he will piece his team together.

His Tar Heels are in Maui, having cruised past Brigham Young University in the Maui Invitational opener. But now Raymond Felton is in a heap at the top of the key, and from where Williams is standing, it looks like Felton landed on his wrist.

This is much more serious than a silly one-game NCAA suspension. An injury could put Felton on the bench for weeks, or even months. In 1984, when Williams was a Carolina assistant, he watched a Kenny Smith wrist injury derail one of the very best Tar Heel teams ever. Would it happen again? Felton's wrist may be broken, and the replacement options are limited. Quentin Thomas, a freshman, is still licking his wounds from the Santa Clara game. Wes Miller, a transfer from James Madison, has the advantage of a year's worth of practices in the Williams system but is not as good a defender as Felton. Melvin Scott could slide over to point guard, as he did as a freshman, but his niche is shooting.

Felton pulls himself off the Lahaina Civic Center floor and finishes the Tennessee game with 9 points and 9 assists in 33 minutes.

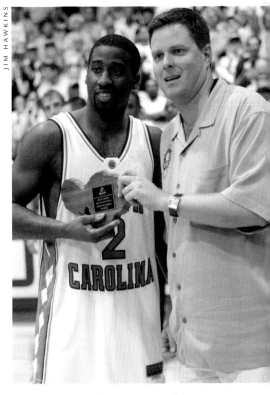

JIM HAWKINS

ESPN interviews May prior to the Maui Invitational (opposite); Felton accepts the tournament MVP trophy (above).

A local doctor examines Felton's wrist after the game. The diagnosis is inconclusive: It's probably not broken, but it could be. It is two more days before the Tar Heels can return home and get a definitive verdict.

"There wasn't a lump in my throat," Roy Williams says. "There was fear in my heart. I didn't want to have to go through playing for an extended period of time without Raymond. The team was not ready to do that."

"I was trying to think of every possibility," assistant coach Joe Holladay says. "I thought we could put a cast on there and maybe he could just play in the games. He doesn't ever have to practice again, just play in the games."

There is no good time for a potentially crushing injury to the point guard. But this timing is especially cruel. The Tar Heels had arrived in Maui to the traditional lei greeting and gorgeous island weather. Their head coach, however, had a message for them:

"We're not in Maui yet."

The tone of his voice was alarming. It canceled all thoughts of snorkeling, all possibilities of lounging on the sand.

"It's like when you know your fate, but you have to wait on it," Jackie Manuel says. "And time is just ticking and ticking."

That first practice in Maui eventually becomes the stuff of legend. Ask any Tar Heel to cite the most important practice session of the year, and they unanimously turn to that one.

McCants averaged 20.7 points in three victories in Maui (opposite); a snorkeling trip on Thanksgiving Day (above); the coaching staff at work (below).

thought for the day

"Not I—but we."

—November 20, 2004

Hours in a stuffy Maui gym, defensive slides, endless sprints. It is not fun. It is not even basketball, really.

It is work.

That's what it is. Roy Williams works his team. They walk out of the gym with shirts wringing wet with sweat, tongues dragging. The message from the head coach is simple: He wants this kind of effort every single day, no matter the opponent. He wants to hammer teams, to play the type of beautiful basketball that makes future opponents click off the television with a sense of foreboding.

His players return to their rooms to marvel at the way they have been pushed. There is a sense of accomplishment but also a sense of fear. Could every practice from now until April be this way? Their head coach has a way of ending particularly rigorous practices with an ominous tone: "If you think today's practice was hard, don't come back tomorrow. It will be tougher."

They believe him.

They do not know that when he returns to his room, Roy Williams is not plotting their destruction in the next practice or planning a two-hour defensive drill.

He is turning to his wife, Wanda, and saying something he would never say to his team: "You know, we could be pretty doggone good."

But the Tar Heels cannot be pretty doggone good, maybe not even plain old good, without Felton. Thankfully, the pinball of a point guard returns to the lineup in the tournament championship game against Iowa. He comes out

Freshmen Thomas and M. Williams on the beach (above); the team and staff hang ten (below); Scott, who scored in double figures in tournament games vs. BYU and Tennessee, connects from the corner vs. Iowa (opposite, Nov. 24).

for early pregame warm-ups favoring his wrist, not touching the ball at all with his left hand. But for the second warm-ups, with just three minutes before tip-off, he ditches that plan. He dribbles left-handed, shoots left-handed. He will play.

He doesn't just play—he excels. With his injured wrist heavily wrapped, he hands out 9 assists, commits just 1 turnover, and grabs 4 steals while spending part of the game defending the Hawkeyes' ace scorer, Jeff Horner.

Felton wins the tournament MVP award; Carolina wins its first championship of any kind since the preseason NIT two seasons before. Santa Clara seems like a distant memory.

"The guys knew they had to respond [to the Santa Clara loss] in a very favorable way," assistant coach Steve Robinson says. "Respond didn't necessarily mean winning games, but that there had to be a better collective effort from everyone involved, in practice and in games. There had to be more attention to detail. And those guys did that. They responded."

The verdict on Felton's wrist comes in after the team returns to Chapel Hill: not broken, just a sprain. He will have to play with a heavy wrap for several weeks, but he will play.

The pieces still fit.

Felton's impressive dunk helped seal the Maui title against Iowa (opposite); Carolina defeated BYU, Tennessee, and Iowa by a combined 63 points (above); J. Williams scored 18 points in the title game (right).

The Silence & the Roar

CHAPTER THREE

The crowd is a living thing.

Not the individuals, but the cumulative mass made up of the thousands of fans that pack into every North Carolina basketball game. It's alive. Really. Carolina's players and coaches know it, know it as surely as they know that the basket is 10 feet high and the court is 94 feet long. They know that a supportive crowd can push them, can add an extra inch to their leap or an extra gulp of breath in their lungs. And they know that a harsh opposing crowd can suck the life out of a team.

In the span of about 64 hours following a home opener win over Southern Cal, the Tar Heels draw enough energy from crowds—in two completely different ways—to notch their two biggest nonconference wins of the pre-Christmas slate.

The 70-63 win at Indiana gets little national attention. The Hoosiers are in a down year and will eventually finish a meager 15-14, out of the NCAA Tournament. A win over a .500 team is ordinarily not cause for celebration.

May dunks in his homecoming at Assembly Hall in Bloomington (Dec. 1, opposite); J. Williams had 13 points and 6 rebounds in the win at Indiana (right).

J. D. LYON JR.

13

But this is not just a win over a .500 team. It is a win on the road in one of the most difficult environments the Tar Heels will face all year, against a coach and a crowd with something to prove.

Indiana's 17,257-seat Assembly Hall looks like it was built to meet central casting's demand for a typical Midwestern field house. The seats on the side of the court ascend at a steep grade, so that even fans on the upper rows appear to be right on top of the court. Indiana doesn't bother with most of the fancy pyrotechnics the Tar Heels see at other road arenas. No smoke-spewing motorcycles riding onto the court, no dancing mascot, no pumped-in techno music over the PA system. The atmosphere is created solely by the fans and the pep band.

It is the least glitzy road environment Carolina faces during the 2004–05 season. It is also the best.

Lubed by an intense dislike of Carolina junior Sean May, a Bloomington native whose father was a Hoosier star and National Player of the Year, the crowd arrives early and locks in on May immediately. He hears chants of "traitor" and derogatory comments about his father. This is the kind of atmosphere in which Carolina teams of the recent past have become extremely brittle. The results in previous road games are not pretty: The Tar Heels are 8–25 over their last 33 true road games.

"I was a nervous wreck playing on the road our first couple of years," Jackie Manuel says. "It was tough: people screaming at you and yelling at you and there are cameras on you. But we're older now. We've learned from our

ROBERT CRAWFORD

McCants scored a season-high 28 points vs. Kentucky (Dec. 4, opposite); Noel scored 10 points off the bench against the Wildcats (above).

Despite playing with a severely sprained left wrist, Felton had 7 assists vs. Kentucky (above); McCants made key baskets and 10 of 11 free throws (opposite).

PEYTON WILLIAMS

mistakes. And now we understand the fans can't do anything. The rims are the same size. Last year, we'd go on the road and the other team would go on a run and it was like the game was over. This year when we go on the road, if the other team goes on a run, it doesn't matter to us. We know we'll get our run eventually."

It is not a particularly artistic run, but it is effective. Despite a scoring drought of 5:14 late in the second half, the Tar Heels and their prodigal son survive.

Indiana makes the game interesting until the final minute, draining four three-pointers in the closing two minutes, but never gets closer than 5 points. With 22.9 seconds left and Carolina holding an 8-point lead, Sean May leaves the floor on which he spent much of his childhood. He has heard jeers for most of the night. This time, he hears something much more gratifying.

"Coach Williams always says it's the best thing in the world to hear the other team's fans get quiet," May says. "I first started noticing it with about a minute left, and it felt great."

Three days later the Tar Heels are the beneficiary of a rowdy crowd. Kentucky is Carolina's most heated nonconference rival, and the Wildcats have owned the recent series between the two programs. Revenge is in the air as 21,750 fans squeeze into the Smith Center and produce one of the most intense home atmospheres of the Roy Williams era. Chapel Hill crowds drew some deserved criticism in the mid- to late-1990s. But the 8–20 season snapped some of the entitlement mind-set, and winning is once again fun at Carolina.

"I'm convinced our team was focused before the Kentucky game, but I'm even more convinced our crowd raised our level of play a little bit early," Roy Williams says. "We got off to a good start because we were so active defensively. We got a lot of that energy from the crowd. It was no wine and cheese crowd in the Smith Center."

The Heels coast in for a therapeutic 91–78 victory. They have exorcised road demons. They have exorcised Kentucky Wildcat demons. And they have proven that they know how to work a crowd.

Building a Program

CHAPTER FOUR

The line begins outside the Smith Center at 6:45 A.M. on December 31, 2004.

Carolina's players won't be in the building for at least another three hours, but that doesn't stop the crowd from growing.

It's not even game day. It's clinic day.

The Rams Club, Carolina's athletic fund-raising organization, holds a series of meetings around the state each spring. Roy Williams was a featured speaker throughout the 2003 meetings, and he harped on one particular talking point at each stop: "I'm not just trying to build a team. I'm trying to build a program."

BOB DONNAN

Manuel drives to the basket (opposite); McCants contributes to Carolina's 49-point win over Loyola (Dec. 12, right), the largest margin of the season.

JEFFREY A. CAMARATI

The annual holiday clinic is a highlight for Carolina players and coaches (above); Felton and his teammates welcomed Virginia Tech to the ACC with a 34-point victory over the Hokies (Dec. 19, right).

For Williams, the quality team is born of the quality program. His definition of program success includes such measurables as NCAA Tournament appearances, victories, and championships, but it also relies on a few less tangible aspects. That's why only a day after whitewashing Cleveland State 107–64 at the Smith Center, his players are straggling back into the building for the annual kids' clinic.

The Carolina team is not tested much in the 33 days after the win over Kentucky. The Tar Heels post six wins by an average of 34 points each in that span. Only one of those games, a 93–65 win over Vermont, is against an NCAA Tournament team. The other notable victory is an 85–51 thrashing of Virginia Tech in Blacksburg—the Hokies' inauguration into Atlantic Coast Conference basketball.

But while the team is coasting, the program is building. The month around the holidays traditionally marks some of Williams's most important community efforts. The coaches and players deliver turkeys to shelters and the Ronald McDonald House at Thanksgiving, an event sponsored in part by former Tar Heels Jerry Stackhouse and Antawn Jamison. The team hosts a clinic for Special Olympians from across the state of North

GRANT HALVERSON

Terry and Scott shop for Christmas gifts (above); Miller scored a season-high 6 points vs. Cleveland State (Dec. 30, right).

Carolina, an event for which participants regularly make a 10-hour round-trip just for 2 hours of instruction. Before Christmas Williams takes the team shopping for underprivileged families, and it's not a simple show-your-face outing—the players are given individual shopping lists, requiring them to put some thought into their purchases and stay within budget. The hypercompetitive players turn it into a contest, as every Tar Heel stands by the cash register to determine which player has gotten closest to the limit without going over, Bob Barker–style. (Sean May claims the victory, although Wes Miller and video coordinator Eric Hoots contend they're the winners.)

And on this New Year's Eve day, the team hosts a children's clinic. The event is only lightly promoted, as organizers fear that heavy promotion would result in an unmanageable crowd. Still, enough information about the clinic leaks to prompt enterprising parents to roust their children from bed in time to be in the Smith Center parking lot at dawn, despite the fact that the clinic doesn't officially begin until 9:00 A.M.

The hundreds of kids who participate get a rare look at the Tar Heels behind the scenes. Most of the players are naturals at interacting with the first-through eighth-graders. Just as tellingly, the players are naturals at interacting with each other. That wasn't always the case last season; this year, however, everyone on the roster genuinely appears to enjoy his teammates' company.

Rookie Marvin Williams prompts the biggest laugh of the day. Assistant coach Joe Holladay drafts Williams into the finals of the "bacon drill" event.

It's exactly how it sounds—participants must simulate a piece of bacon by lying on the floor and shaking their limbs, as if they are sizzling. Williams proves to be a quick study, but not quick enough to emerge victorious.

After three hours of instruction, Roy Williams gives his players a surprising choice. Team practice is still scheduled for the afternoon. But if they perform a song, as a group, over the Smith Center PA for the benefit of the kids, he'll cancel practice.

A huddle ensues. As usual in these entertaining situations, David Noel emerges as the chorus leader, needing only a baton to look every bit the part of a conductor. His "Singing Tar Heels" perform a harmony version—not good harmony, but harmony—of the Barney theme song. Their coach guffaws. Players slap high-fives with each other.

Practice is canceled.

Granted a reprieve from the day's scheduled events, the players could be forgiven for scattering away from basketball. Instead, some linger on the Smith Center floor, working on shooting form. Some hang out in the locker room.

It is not so much what they are doing as how they are doing it—together, as a team—that makes an impression.

Roy Williams is intent on building a program. As he well knows, that goal usually has a beneficial by-product: building a team.

PEYTON WILLIAMS

The Difference of Defense

ROBERT CRAWFORD

Roy Williams wants his team to play fast.

He talks about tempo constantly and can frequently be seen on the sideline waving his arms in a "speed it up" motion. He wants to create turnovers, push the ball, and force the score into the 90s or higher.

His constant emphasis on speed can create the misperception that Carolina is just a helter-skelter offensive team lucky enough to outscore opponents on a regular basis. In reality, the Tar Heels run a precise offense that relies on endless reads and adjustments. The point guard must constantly evaluate and react to movements on the floor; his decisions are made more critical by the frenetic pace and the need to flow immediately from the fast break into the secondary break, the backbone of a high-scoring attack.

The team executes well. From December 12 to January 12, they blow past the competition, scoring at least 91 points in seven of eight games. But the high-octane offense is just a smokescreen for the real key to a Roy Williams attack: 50 feet of lockdown, arm-waving, suffocating defense.

Terry scored a season-high 11 points against Maryland (Jan. 8, opposite); M. Williams had 12 points and 9 boards vs. the Terrapins (right).

25

thought for the day

"The higher you go, the more dependent you are on others."

—January 10, 2005

J. Williams scored 18 points in the win over No. 8 Georgia Tech (Jan. 12, left); May and Luke Schenscher battle near the rim (opposite).

ROBERT CRAWFORD

Unlike some of his coaching brethren who prefer to pair fast-paced offense with a full-court pressing defense, Williams has never been a proponent of the full-court press. He does believe, however, in applying constant pressure as soon as the ball crosses the midcourt line. He cited defense as his biggest preseason concern and has hammered it home in practice every day since October 16.

His team is getting the message.

"We had a bunch of guys who are very talented individuals," assistant coach Steve Robinson says. "All of them were probably big scorers on their high school team. A lot of them probably weren't asked to be a defensive player."

They're not *asked* to be defensive players at Carolina. They're required to be.

Before the January 8 matchup with Maryland, some doubts about the Tar Heels remain. Carolina stands 12–1 with a 12-game winning streak, but they haven't been tested since the Kentucky game more than a month before. Skeptics refuse to anoint them a powerful team until the Heels face quality competition.

Those skeptics fade in the fury of two of Carolina's most impressive ACC games since the 1993 championship squad.

Again, it's offense that draws attention as the Tar Heels embarrass Maryland 109–75 and pound Georgia Tech 91–69. The Heels are a running, gunning, fun-to-watch machine that destroys two of the ACC's best programs. Carolina shoots 56.5 percent against the Terps and routs Tech 46–28 in the first half, eventually winning the game by 22 points.

But offense is not what Roy Williams notices. He notices the way Raymond Felton controls John Gilchrist and Jarrett Jack, holding them to a combined 4 assists and pressuring them into 8 turnovers. Williams values the point guard more highly than any other position on the floor. That position initiates his hyperkinetic offense, of course, but a skilled

PEYTON WILLIAMS

point guard can do something more—stifle the other team's offense. Felton is becoming that player. He won five straight team defensive awards in December and will win nine for the season, second only to Jackie Manuel's 14.

Felton is deceptively strong, possessing enough upper body strength to dish out as much punishment as he takes. Teammates look to him to set the tone defensively, and when he hunches over, lips pursed, eyes locked on his man while clapping his hands as the opposing point guard crosses the midcourt line, Carolina becomes a fearsome defensive squad.

There are other subtle signs of improvement: the way the team dominates the Jackets on the boards (holding a 52–33 rebounding advantage); the way Maryland musters just 2-for-22 from beyond the three-point line.

For the first time in his tenure at Carolina, Roy Williams decides that he may have the makings of a formidable defensive team. That's the foundation of the 14-game winning streak the Tar Heels ride into mid-January.

"Some of those teams we might have beaten last year by 20," Jawad Williams says. "But we should have beaten them by 30 or 40. Last year we had lapses where we didn't get stops on defense. We took it for granted. This year we played defense, and that's what helped us in those games."

Even the powerful 1998 squad had only three 20-plus point ACC victories in the regular season. The 2005 Tar Heels already have three, and they've done it in just three league contests.

"We weren't just beating people," David Noel says. "We were beating people badly. And we got a little swagger about us, and then we were rolling."

Felton was one of seven double-figure scorers in the win over Maryland (opposite); Felton guards John Gilchrist (above); May blocks a Maryland shot (right).

JEFFREY A. CAMARATI

JEFFREY A. CAMARATI

PEYTON WILLIAMS

The Blue Team

CHAPTER SIX

For some Tar Heels, progress is judged by the bottom of the daily practice plan.

It's just one sheet of paper—a thought for the day and offensive and defensive emphasis at the top, followed by the practice schedule broken down into exact times: "4:42 shooting form, 4:48 fast break drill #1."

The bottom of the page is where subtle rewards can be found. The practice plan first lists the White team, the squad essentially made up of the rotation regulars. Only five players take the court at a time, but the White squad can comprise five to ten players—the starters and their substitutes. The Blue team, one of the most famous Dean Smith innovations, is listed next. Odds are that the Blue squad members won't play many meaningful minutes in the next game. But because of Smith, it's almost a badge of honor. The legendary former Tar Heel coach occasionally substituted five members of the Blue team at one time. He'd do it when he thought his starters lacked energy, or when he wanted to rest the members of the rotation, or when he simply wanted a quick burst of all-out effort.

JEFFREY A. CAMARATI

Sanders scored 22 points and had 23 rebounds as a junior (opposite); Everett in action (right).

PEYTON WILLIAMS

JIM HAWKINS

JEFFREY A. CAMARATI

BOB DONNAN

The increase in television timeouts has negated much of the Blue team's strategic importance. With a two-minute timeout for every four minutes of clock action, fatigue is not as big a factor in college basketball games. Carolina hasn't regularly used a true Blue team in several years.

Nevertheless, players see the assignment as a challenge. Throughout much of the season, athletic sophomore Reyshawn Terry checks the practice plan for signs of his progress. On occasion, after a particularly impressive effort, Roy Williams elevates Terry to the White team as a reward. It is a powerful incentive.

"He talked to me during the season and told me moving to the White team could be motivation for me," Terry says. "If I made the White, that meant I was really making progress. That helped me stay motivated and kept me working hard."

The Blue team makes most of its contributions in practice. Wes Miller and Quentin Thomas harass Raymond Felton every day; C. J. Hooker, Charlie Everett, and Byron Sanders bang with Sean May, Jawad Williams, and Marvin

thought for the day

"Have you made your teammates better today?"

—November 3, 2004

Miller, Terry, Foster, and Hooker contribute on the court (opposite, clockwise from top left); Thomas and Holley focus on the basket (below).

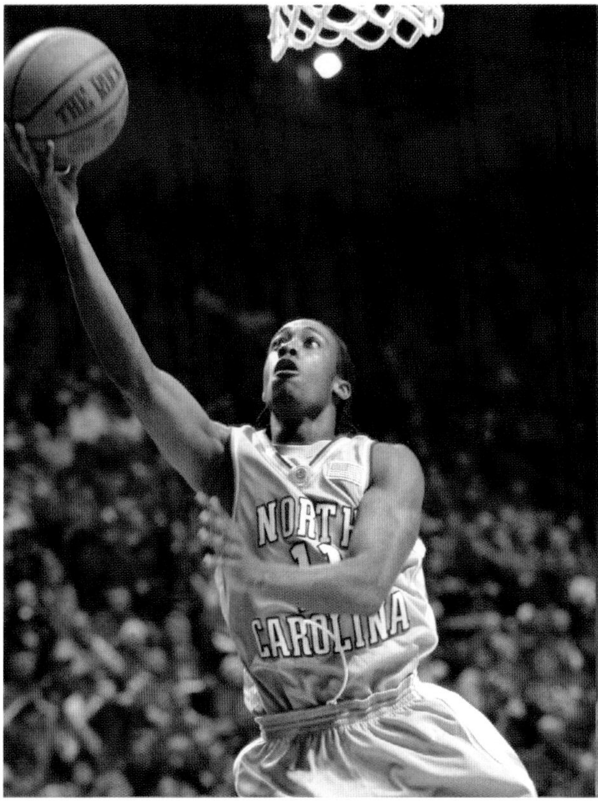

JIM HAWKINS

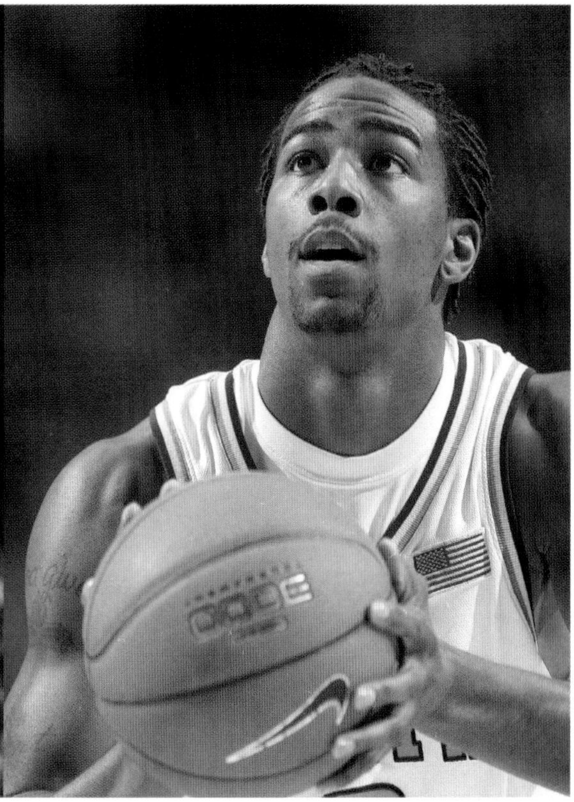

PEYTON WILLIAMS

JEFFREY A. CAMARATI

Williams in the post. The Tar Heels even get a boost from the football squad, as wide receivers Jesse Holley and Brooks Foster join the basketball team and provide valuable depth and athleticism.

"I look at it two ways," Miller says. "Number one, I want to contribute to this team just as much as I possibly can. I want to have an impact and help this team and whole staff win. This year my goal in practice was to push the White team, specifically pushing Raymond. I also looked at it as a chance for me to improve. I got to play against the best point guard in the country every day and that can prepare me for next year."

The mind-set of a Blue team player is tricky. He must accept his limited role but also be prepared to enter the game at any time. When Roy Williams gets frustrated with his starters, he sometimes walks the length of the bench, seemingly gauging the potential impact of each of the players he finds there. Sometimes, the call comes quickly.

That's what happens for Terry in the January 8 win over Maryland. He is inserted for a listless Rashad McCants and immediately helps the Heels recover from a 29–24 deficit. The Winston-Salem native scores on a drive, plays quality defense, tips out an offensive rebound, and hits a three-pointer.

JEFFREY A. CAMARATI

Grant looks for the ball (above); Sanders gets a bucket (left).

Those plays create a dramatic momentum shift, and the game eventually turns into a blowout. The Blue team accumulates some minutes as a unit, with the highlight being a Thomas-to-Terry alley-oop.

For Thomas, it's the perfect example of life as a Blue team player. Two days earlier, he had gone through an extremely rough practice, drawing the ire of Roy Williams for failing to pick up difficult concepts and provide enough resistance to Felton. But Felton—who has served as a mentor to Thomas, counseling him on every nuance of the point-guard position—picks up his third foul with 15:43 left in the Maryland game, and Thomas steps in for five solid minutes of relief, increasing the Tar Heel lead.

"I just try to learn," Thomas says. "I know this whole year is going to be a learning experience for me. Coach is on everybody, but of course he's going to be on his point guards because we have to be a coach on the floor. The main thing is to listen to Coach Williams and run the way he wants to run, but at the same time I have to play basketball and play off my instincts. It makes me better."

Full substitution: Holley, Thomas, Everett, Hooker, and Miller prepare to enter the national semifinals vs. Michigan State.

History Repeats Itself

CHAPTER SEVEN

JIM HAWKINS

As the train that was Atlantic Coast Conference expansion thundered toward its ultimate conclusion— Virginia Tech and the University of Miami joining the league for the 2004–05 basketball season, Boston College joining a year later—most of the talk was about football.

The growth from 9 teams to 12 teams meant the addition of a lucrative conference championship game. Miami's powerful program combined with the presence of Florida State gave the league a major foothold in the state of Florida. The ACC would finally have enough prestigious programs to challenge the Southeastern Conference for football supremacy in the Southeast.

North Carolina and Duke were the least enthu-siastic of all conference schools during expansion discussions. For Carolina, there were two major concerns: finances

Despite Manuel's efforts, the Tar Heels trailed by 10 at halftime against Wake Forest (Jan. 15, opposite); M. Williams's 15 points and 7 rebounds weren't enough to win in Winston-Salem (right).

and scheduling. UNC had always eschewed corporate signage, which meant that the conference financial package was of primary importance. And Tar Heel administrators worried about the damage that expansion could do to ACC basketball, a product that had thrived for 50 years on a full round-robin schedule. Lose to a team on the road in early January, and there was a chance to avenge the defeat at home in late February. But with 11 or 12 league teams instead of 9, a full double round-robin wasn't feasible. It simply would not provide enough flexibility to schedule marquee nonconference opponents.

The loss of the double round-robin went largely unmourned outside Chapel Hill. Until the third Saturday in January.

On January 15 the Tar Heels travel to Winston-Salem for the season's only meeting between two of the top five teams in the nation.

It is the first time since 1922 that the old rivals will not play a home-and-home, and it causes some consternation among fans who have been spoon-fed the ACC party line on expansion.

The game doesn't do much to make the Carolina faithful feel better. In front of a bouncing, boisterous crowd, the Deacons capture a 95–82 victory that gives them the early lead in the conference championship race.

Wake's game plan is simple: Send constant double-teams at Carolina post players and force Jawad Williams, Marvin Williams, and Sean May to pass out of trouble. The Tar Heels might beat them. But the Deacons aren't going to let the big men beat them.

It is a risky strategy, but the Deacons get an important break when Rashad McCants picks up his fourth foul only a minute into the second half. McCants is the main perimeter outlet for forwards under pressure. An impending double-team in the post means that a Tar Heel is open elsewhere; it usually takes only a swing pass or two to find McCants unguarded for a three-pointer. But with him on the bench, UNC's offensive options shrivel.

"When Rashad is on the floor, he takes a lot of the attention," May says. "You take him out of the game and you miss his presence."

With McCants out and the Deacons neutralizing Carolina post players, Raymond Felton feels compelled to try and take over the offense. He falls into

too much one-on-one play against Wake point guard extraordinaire Chris Paul and takes a whopping 18 shots, more than he attempts in any other game during the season.

May and Wake Forest's Chris Paul were the USA Basketball Co-Players of the Year in 2004.

When he gathers his team in the Lawrence Joel Coliseum locker room after the game, Roy Williams's message is simple: "Guys, we made too many mistakes trying to go one-on-one. We did not play our game. You can't just talk it. You've got to go out on the floor and do it. Today we spent more time talking than we spent doing it."

In certain circles, it is considered a watershed game. Some national columnists label the 2005 Tar Heels the same old Carolina team from the past few years, doing the same old thing—falling apart in a big game. For the first time in several seasons, though, the Tar Heel players don't seem to believe it. There is no finger-pointing in the locker room, no miffed stares on the bus ride home.

"We were upset because it was the first time we wouldn't get another chance at them later in the year," Jackie Manuel says. "But it was a game we needed. We had won 14 games in a row, everybody was talking about it, and maybe we started thinking we were pretty big. I didn't want to lose. But we needed to be brought back down to earth."

Awards & Rewards

They are an interesting bunch, these 2004–05 Tar Heels.

From a personality standpoint, certainly. And in terms of team composition.

College basketball has undergone such a dramatic change over the previous decade that it's unlikely Carolina will field a team like this again. It is a rarity today—an upperclassmen-dominated team. Players with raw talent and NBA aspirations usually do not stay in school long enough to declare a major. For a variety of reasons, and due to a variety of circumstances, the Tar Heels' most talented juniors and seniors are still in Chapel Hill.

They are an eclectic group. Sean May's father is extremely involved in his career; Melvin Scott's father passed away before he enrolled at Carolina. Jawad Williams is from a tough section of Cleveland where strangers don't speak unless they want trouble; Raymond Felton is from

May's 17 points and 15 rebounds helped Carolina overcome a sloppy first half vs. Miami (Jan. 22, opposite); McCants and his fellow starters all scored in double figures against the Hurricanes (right).

BOB DONNAN

thought for the day

"Stormy weather is what man needs from time to time to remind him he is really not in charge of anything."

—January 18, 2005

a small town in South Carolina where strangers feel it's their right, maybe even their obligation, to treat him as a favored son. Marvin Williams says he occasionally needs a day off from basketball and can get burned out on the sport; Rashad McCants thinks about the game constantly.

Somehow, though, they fit. That hasn't always been the case. Some very un-Carolina-like mind-sets formed during the dark times of 2001–02 and during the team's NIT appearance the next season. With wins scarce, players began aiming for individual accomplishments as a way to make coming to practice feel worthwhile. *We can't win? Well, then I'll go out and get 20 points to make myself feel good.* At times they paid more attention to the shot-attempts stat line than the final score.

Most of that dissension dissolves over the summer of 2004. David Noel has been working on his shooting, but once the season begins, he realizes that his offense is less important than his defense and dedicates himself to being "this year's Jackie Manuel"—the Carolina way of saying he wants to be an ace defender. Scott goes from a starting role as a junior to a bench slot as a senior and his minutes are halved, but he never publicly complains. Jawad Williams, who occasionally engaged in a test of wills with McCants in previous years, begins echoing the "Winners get awards and

Michael Jordan holds a shooting contest with the Heels (below); Noel played an outstanding all-around game vs. NC State (Feb. 3, opposite).

JEFFREY A. CAMARATI

rewards" line preached by Roy Williams and expresses no qualms about McCants being the designated late-game go-to offensive player.

The new team-first approach makes the Tar Heels especially dangerous. They're no longer just a collection of talented individuals—they function as a whole. If one part is misfiring, the others compensate.

After the tough loss to Wake Forest, they rededicate themselves to this principle and start another winning streak, this time posting five straight ACC victories by an average of 23.6 points per game. Included in this run is a 110–76 thrashing of Virginia in which the Heels lead by 50 points, 98–48, with five minutes left on the game clock. It is the program's first win in Charlottesville since 1999.

The stark differences from last year crystallize in Tallahassee. In January 2004 the Tar Heels suffered an embarrassing loss there when the Seminoles clawed back from a 24-point deficit to claim the victory in overtime. The 'Noles make another comeback this year, drawing to 49–48 with 14:16 left after trailing early by 18.

Roy Williams does not call a timeout, instead preferring to let his veteran squad work through its struggles. The Tar Heels go to a favorite play, a box setup with several options. The cleanest and most emphatic option comes open immediately: Rashad McCants slips free behind the Florida State defense for an alley-oop slam dunk.

Point made. Comeback thwarted. "This has gotten to be a very mature bunch," Roy Williams says after the game, and it is perhaps the best compliment he could give his team.

During the conference winning stretch, four different Tar Heels lead the team in scoring. The two-time leader is McCants, who posts a team-high 23 points at Clemson and 16 at Florida State. Even so, his scoring average is down. He is a basketball player, and all basketball players want points—but it's worth noting that his assist numbers have sharply increased while his turnovers have decreased. McCants will end the season with a positive assist/turnover ratio for the first time in his career. With this achievement comes a new appreciation for the game.

"Everyone on this team loves to be around each other," McCants says. "Practices are so live and enjoyable. You feel something really special with this team. I don't think I've ever had this much fun playing basketball."

M. Williams dunks at Florida State
in one of the most memorable plays
of the season (Feb. 6, opposite).

The Perils of Hesitation

Coaches are copiers.

Although the self-deprecating Tar Heel head coach has made more adjustments than he'll admit to the Dean Smith blueprint, Roy Williams claims to be more of a copier than an innovator.

So it's not surprising that in January 1993, after Williams's Kansas team (which eventually lost to Carolina in the Final Four) was defeated by Long Beach State, the coach took a page from his opponent's book. He adapted a play that Long Beach used frequently during its 64–49 victory over the Jayhawks and added it to his team's end-of-game strategy. The beauty of the play is its multiple options: It allows for post-up opportunities, perimeter jump shots, and even dribble penetration. It's the job of the point guard to read the defense—split-second decision making is a necessity—and determine which particular option is available.

Williams imported the play to Chapel Hill when he arrived, and the Tar Heels used it successfully in two crucial situations during his

ROBERT CRAWFORD

M. Williams defends DeMarcus Nelson in the loss at Duke (Feb. 9, opposite); May tallied 23 points and 18 boards vs. the Blue Devils (right).

47

first season—once to create a Jawad Williams dunk that tied the home game against Wake Forest, and once to create a Rashad McCants three-pointer that beat Connecticut.

On February 9, 2005, the Tar Heels trail Duke 71–70 but have possession of the ball with 18 seconds to play. The play call is clear: Long Beach.

Carolina has performed poorly, turning the ball over 23 times in a low-possession game. Duke hits 21 of 22 free throws, and Carolina shoots just 3 of 14 from the three-point line. But Sean May piles up 23 points and 18 rebounds, and offense isn't even his most impressive contribution. He dominates Shelden Williams defensively, pushing the talented Duke center away from the basket and holding Williams without a field goal attempt in the second half.

So the game is somehow winnable, and the last play call is obvious. Maybe too obvious. Duke's J. J. Redick will say later that the Blue Devils anticipated that exact set, and the Devils defend it well. As Redick shadows McCants around a screen and denies the ball on the left wing, McCants thinks, "They know what the play is."

There are several other options on the set, but as Felton dribbles, all of them evaporate. Duke cuts off Marvin Williams in the paint, May can't slip the screen he set for McCants, and the clock is under five seconds.

Felton spent most of his high school career and his first year at Carolina in a freewheeling offense designed to cater to his skills. He is dynamic on the fast break. "I just see things before they happen," he once explained. "I can throw the ball before my teammate is there because I know what he's going to do and what the defenders are going to do."

His first year under Roy Williams, however, was a learning experience. Williams teaches a fast tempo, but it's not an unrestrained tempo. The offense relies on precise decision making from the point guard. At times during his sophomore year, Felton struggled with those decisions. Now, as a junior on Duke's home court, he tries to do exactly what his coach asks of him, to run plays exactly as they are diagrammed.

Duke makes a mistake. Daniel Ewing overplays and goes for a steal, taking him out of the play and leaving Felton momentarily uncovered. Felton peers into the lane, sees open space between himself and the foul line. It is a situation Carolina covered the day before in practice. "If it's there," Roy

Williams told him, "go ahead and take it."

As 9,314 souls stand and scream in Cameron Indoor Stadium, one of the loudest buildings the Heels will play in all year, Felton sees something: It is there, if only for a sliver of a second. But he does not take it. That's not the first option of the designed play, not the way the Tar Heels ran it when it worked so well against Wake and UConn the year before.

The point guard hesitates. In that moment, the opening vanishes. Felton tries to shovel the ball to Noel near the sideline. Noel bobbles it, and the ball trickles out of bounds as the clock expires.

In the immediate aftermath, Felton is his own harshest critic. Teammates and coaches try to assume some of the blame in the cramped visiting team locker room, but Felton shrugs them off. The ball was in his hands. Eighteen seconds, one point. The game was winnable.

"It was the third time we'd been to Durham and been inches from winning the game," Felton says. "I was thinking, 'Not again.' It's so tough knowing we could have beaten them every time we've played over there and we didn't come through with it."

Felton finishes with 3 assists, 8 turnovers, and one mistake for which he can't forgive himself.

It becomes the turning point of the season.

ROBERT CRAWFORD

Felton scored 13 points at Duke, but it was the play he failed to make at the end of the game that turned Carolina's season around.

49

Back on Track

CHAPTER TEN

The Tar Heels are beaten, they are bruised, and they are sick.

They have lost a 1-point game to their most bitter rival. A variety of players are nursing the types of nicks that accumulate during the rigors of an ACC season, and a wicked virus is making its way through the team. The squad flies to Connecticut for a nonconference interlude, a trip that includes a stop at the ESPN studios for a quick tour.

How sick are some of the players? David Noel, perhaps the most natural television star of anyone on the roster, skips the tour and goes straight to his hotel room. Several of his teammates, including Jackie Manuel (who will throw up on the sidelines during the first half of Sunday's game) and Sean May are battling flu-like symptoms.

STEVE KIRSCHNER

May had 16 points and a game-high 13 rebounds at UConn (Feb. 13, opposite), one of his 18 double-doubles on the year; Manuel and J. Williams try out the SportsCenter set at the ESPN studios (right).

J.D. LYON JR.

thought for the day

"Good teams have good players. GREAT teams have GREAT teammates."

—February 15, 2005

The Tar Heels will face the defending national champions on their home court. A losing streak seems imminent.

But Roy Williams is learning how to handle his team. When he first came to UNC, there were two distinct sides—players and coaches—and neither group seemed completely sure of how to respond to the other. By February 13, the day of the Connecticut game, that sort of disconnect is ancient history. Team practices are intense but not tense, a change from last year, when an explosion always seemed possible. Prepractice shooting and stretching drills are usually filled with laughter and good-natured joking. When the players split up at the beginning of each practice, guards go to one end of the floor with assistant coach Steve Robinson. They begin their day by rhythmically bouncing basketballs in tandem, usually culminating with the latest dance stylings of Melvin Scott.

The chemistry among team members gives the Tar Heels a bit of a rough edge. Any criticism by outsiders serves as a rallying point. The perception now is that Carolina can't win a big road game. They have failed in road tests at Wake Forest and Duke. Surely they will go to Hartford and suffer another disappointment.

Raymond Felton plays in a post-Duke funk in the first half,

struggling defensively against Connecticut point guard Marcus Williams. "Raymond was still feeling the impact of the other night in the first half," Roy Williams later reflects. "He felt like he didn't make a play down the stretch and that was bothering him."

His second-half play, however, foreshadows the point guard who will eventually lead the Tar Heels to a title. The smallest player on the court scores, passes, and is poised at all times. UConn's Charlie Villanueva slams home a dunk to trim the Carolina lead to 58–54 with under nine minutes to play, sparking a roar from the 16,294 fans in attendance, a growing crescendo that threatens to swallow the Tar Heels—but there is Felton, an unruffled look on his face as he prepares to receive the inbounds pass. He holds his hands out to his teammates, palms toward the floor. "Calm down," he seems to be saying. "We've got this."

They do get it, a 77–70 hard-earned victory. Jawad Williams emerges from a minislump with 17 big points. The senior does it not by ignoring the pressure, but by relishing it.

Detroit Piston Rasheed Wallace greets Coach Williams before the UConn game (opposite); McCants powers through the lane (right).

"I respond better under pressure," he says. "When I get put in tough situations, I come out on top. So when I put more pressure on myself, I perform at a high level. I called home before that game and told my mother, sister, and dad that if I didn't play well in the UConn game, we were going to lose. That pressure to perform was there, and I responded."

There is only one small note of concern as the Heels roll forward, notching blowout wins over Virginia and Clemson. Something is amiss with Rashad McCants, who doesn't look comfortable with his shot. He made just 3 of 13 attempts at Duke, 7 of 16 at UConn, and 3 of 9 against Clemson. Given that he is one of the purest shooters ever to play at Carolina, these struggles raise some eyebrows. Even alum George Lynch, now in the NBA, phones the UNC basketball office, offering a few technical pointers for the junior.

"When Rashad gets that elbow underneath [his shot] and shoots, I think it's going in every time," Roy Williams says. It is not going in as frequently. And it will be three weeks before the coach sees the familiar form again.

Felton had 16 points, 10 assists, and 2 turnovers at UConn (opposite); J. Williams contributes to Carolina's third straight win over the Huskies (right).

J. D. LYON JR.

Road
Warriors

Injuries are a part of Carolina basketball history.

The 1977 team was decimated by injuries to Tommy LaGarde, Walter Davis, and Phil Ford, ultimately perhaps costing the Tar Heels a national championship. The 1984 squad was cruising along at 17–0 before Kenny Smith broke his wrist against LSU.

The team's chemistry was never the same, and Indiana upset the Heels in the NCAA Tournament. James Worthy broke his ankle in 1980; Steve Hale broke his collarbone in 1985.

Never before, however, has an intestinal disorder been such a cause for concern. Team doctors inform Roy Williams before an away game at NC State that sharpshooter Rashad McCants is out

Scott celebrates the three-pointer that gave Carolina a 38–33 halftime lead at NC State (Feb. 22, opposite). Felton had 21 points, 7 assists, and 0 turnovers against the Wolfpack (right).

KEVIN COX / WIRE IMAGE

indefinitely. Tests are needed, significant rest is required. No definitive timeline is given—he could be out for a week or for the rest of the season.

Two big road tests are looming. First is a trip to the RBC Center in Raleigh, home of perennial Tar Heel thorn Julius Hodge. Then a journey to the Comcast Center, the arena Sean May calls the toughest in the ACC for a visiting team, to face Maryland.

McCants's presence will be missed. He is Carolina's best perimeter scorer, and potential fill-in Melvin Scott is struggling with his shot. The senior guard has not made a three-pointer in the past four games.

"When I shoot the ball and I think too much, I'm always going to miss it," Scott says. "I was thinking too much. But I knew our backs were against the wall. Rashad was out. There was nothing for me to do but play and make shots."

He makes them, nailing two three-pointers in each half against the Wolfpack. The rest of the Tar Heels follow suit from the perimeter, finishing 10 of 21 from behind the arc. They have no one else with the individual skills of McCants. But they don't try to replace him individually. Instead, everyone contributes—Scott with perimeter marksmanship, May with a double-double (14 points and 12 rebounds), Raymond Felton with 21 points, Jawad Williams with 15 points, Marvin Williams with 14 points, and Reyshawn Terry with 15 solid minutes.

Jackie Manuel and David Noel take a combined two shots and score a combined 2 points. Yet they have perhaps their best effort of the season. Manuel has consistently been Carolina's stopper, a spider-like defender capable of shutting down the other team's best guard. Noel spent most of his sophomore season in the post defending bigger players, but the arrival of Marvin Williams enabled him to shift to the perimeter. He thrives there, providing a more muscular alternative to Manuel's ball-hawking defense. They quickly become a formidable tandem, and on this night they harass Hodge into 7-for-16 shooting and 5 turnovers.

"That's about the best night I could have had," Noel says, dismissing his zero shot attempts. "Guarding Hodge is a test, and I was really focused on defense."

And on being a good teammate. In the second half, rookie Marvin Williams takes a hard foul from Hodge, a play the unflappable Williams seems to barely notice. Noel appears out of nowhere, not looking to provoke Hodge

thought for the day

"At any moment, we must be willing to sacrifice what we are for what we are capable of becoming."

—February 20, 2005

J. Williams dunks 2 of his 15 points in the 81–71 win at NC State (opposite).

59

J. D. LYON JR.

J. Williams scored 21 points in the 85–83 win at Maryland (Feb. 27, above); Noel slams a dunk just before the half (opposite).

but making sure the Wolfpack senior understands that he'll need to go through several Tar Heels to get to Williams.

Roy Williams gathers his squad in the locker room with a sense of pride. "That was a team out there," he tells them. "That was all about the name on the front of your jersey, not the name on the back. That was a team."

As Carolina assistant coach Joe Holladay works his way through four Maryland Terrapin game tapes, he has one simple goal.

At some point in every season, the Tar Heels play a close game against an ACC opponent. Toward the end of such games, when time is short, the score is tight, and the opponent has possession of the ball, Roy Williams usually turns to one of his assistants and asks, "What are they going to run?"

Holladay wants to know the answer. He wants to know everything about the opponents he scouts, wants to be able to think like their head coach. Scouting responsibilities on the Tar Heel staff are broken up by opponent, with each assistant responsible for a group of games. The toughest scouting assignments are teams that change the way they play from year to year. Kentucky made significant changes in 2004-05; the Wildcat report took longer than usual.

Holladay's process is simple. "I like to watch about four tapes and run them back over and over," he says. "I try to find a pattern. I'll make some notes if I see calls, and by 'calls' I mean hand signals or verbal signals you can catch sometimes. I'm trying to figure out how that team is going to play us. Is he going to play us man-to-man, zone, or pressure us? First I want the big picture, and then I'll start breaking it down into tendencies. I want to have a pretty good feeling at the end of the game when it's down to one possession and Coach says, 'What are they going to run?'"

On February 27, that moment comes with seven seconds left on the scoreboard in College Park. A critical three-pointer by Jawad Williams and a lay-up by Felton (this time without hesitation) give the Tar Heels an 85–83 lead with 19 seconds remaining. Maryland takes possession and 12 seconds later calls a timeout.

Holladay knows what the Terps will run. He has watched the tapes, knows their tendencies. He is trying to think not like a Carolina assistant, but

like Maryland head coach Gary Williams. He outlines Maryland's preferred end-game out-of-bounds set to Roy Williams.

He is right. The Terps run the exact play he suspected, and their shot never reaches the rim. May comes from the weak side to block Mike Jones, Manuel secures the basketball, and the Tar Heels clinch another ACC road win.

The win washes away some recent struggles in College Park. Before the game, Roy Williams reminded his team of a 96–56 whitewashing the Terps delivered in 2003. The head coach thought the embarrassing loss had come during the 8–20 season, before the arrival of the heralded recruiting class that included May, McCants, and Felton. Told by the latter two that they were on that team, Williams was surprised. "Those guys beat you by 40?" he asked incredulously.

They did. Carolina's seniors have an even more painful memory: They lost 112–79 in College Park during their freshman season. Jawad Williams has been a special target of Terp fans, as his final college decision was between Maryland and Carolina. Although he makes one of the most important baskets of the game, he claims to get no personal satisfaction.

"It wasn't special for my reasons," he says. "It was special because Rashad didn't play and it showed we were still a team even without our leading scorer playing. I wasn't surprised. When we lose anybody from this team, there's always somebody who can step up. Someone will fill the void."

May does just that when the Tar Heels return home. He scores 32 points and pulls down 12 rebounds in a 91–76 victory over Florida State. The 11–18 Seminoles are pesky, but May makes all 10 of his second-half field goal attempts.

Roy Williams gives his seniors the option of cutting down the Smith Center nets after the game, as the Tar Heels have earned a tie for the regular-season ACC championship. Manuel quickly dismisses the idea. He wants the full title, and he knows that his team can get it with a win against Duke three days later.

May rises above Terrapin forward Travis Garrison (opposite); M. Williams scored 17 in Carolina's victory over Florida State (Mar. 3, above); May posted another double-double vs. the Seminoles (right).

BOB DONNAN

JEFFREY A. CAMARATI

Senior Day

PEYTON WILLIAMS

C H A P T E R   T W E L V E

PEYTON WILLIAMS

Jawad Williams hangs his head during a late-game timeout.

His team trails archrival Duke 73–64 in their second meeting of the season. His story-book ending will not come true. He is going to lose his last home game.

"Get your head up!" his head coach snaps.

Outside the huddle there is a general sense of foreboding. Inside the tight circle there is simply confidence.

"You know when you get that feeling like everything is supposed to be right on this day?" David Noel says. "Like it's always going to turn out right? That's the feeling I had today. And that's the feeling the team had when we came out of the huddle with three minutes left."

A measured comeback begins. A tip-in by Jawad. A steal. Two free throws for Marvin Williams. A three-point play by Sean May.

Raymond Felton makes a free throw, then misses one. Somehow he wriggles through the Blue Devil defenders and tips the miss to Marvin Williams. The amazing freshman from Bremerton, Washington, guides the ball into the basket, and 22,125 voices explode.

Manuel slams one home in the first half against Duke (Mar. 6, opposite); Scott, Manuel, Everett, Hooker, and J. Williams salute the crowd on Senior Day (top); after stealing the ball, Felton signals for a timeout with 27 seconds to play (above).

In the din, a whistle blows. Marvin Williams was fouled. He steps to the free throw line, takes a deep breath, dribbles, spins the ball, taps the tattoo of his mother's name on his left arm, and shoots.

"You just have to focus," Williams says of his free-throw shooting. "If you focus, it will go in."

It is good. After J. J. Redick misses a jumper, the game is over, and the Tar Heels are the regular-season champions. The mood swing is akin to an executioner's reprieve. With three minutes remaining on the game clock, the beloved class of Jawad Williams, Melvin Scott, and Jackie Manuel was headed to a

May had 26 points and 24 rebounds in his final Smith Center game (opposite); M. Williams's game-winning three-point play gave Carolina the ACC regular-season title outright (above).

Fans storm the court after the win over Duke (above); the five Tar Heel seniors (opposite).

Senior Day loss against their biggest adversary. Now these players are taking part in one of the greatest Smith Center celebrations in history.

That's when Jawad Williams has to sit down. His legs won't support him; his head is swimming. All the practices on this court, all the freshman-year struggles. A few feet from where he sits, Carolina got a late three-pointer to beat Binghamton by a single point in 2001. From Binghamton to this. Can you imagine?

"I just had to reflect for a minute," Williams says. "I remember coming in here and losing to Hampton and Davidson. I had to reflect on everything I've been through since I came to Carolina."

Five seniors play their last home game on this day, including Charlie

Everett and C. J. Hooker. This is Hooker's second year in the varsity program, Everett's first. They realize that the bond between Williams, Scott, and Manuel is unique. Only the trio knows what is going through Jawad Williams's mind as he watches the postgame celebration.

Freshman season: the year of disappointments. After fully expecting the NCAA Tournament to be a birthright, he doesn't even bother to watch the selection show. Sometimes he feels so disheartened that he dreads walking across campus.

Sophomore season: the year of drama. Has to mediate numerous player/coaching staff tiffs. He is 19 but feels much older, like the big kid in a room full of toddlers arguing over wooden blocks.

Junior season: the year of injuries. He suffers a broken nose and a concussion and plays in pain for much of the year. His confidence wanes.

Senior season: the year of fun.

People close to Jawad Williams have always hinted that there is a devilish side to him, something behind the almost regal bearing he shows the public. It emerges in his final year. He jokes with teammates in front of the media, pulls practical jokes on them in public. His primary target is Marvin Williams, the easygoing freshman he could have seen as a threat. Instead, the elder player considers him a friend.

"Coming together is a beginning, keeping together is progress, and working together is success."

—March 4, 2005

JEFFREY A. CAMARATI

JAWAD WILLIAMS

PEYTON WILLIAMS   BOB DONNAN

BOB DONNAN   JEFFREY A. CAMARATI

ANDREW WILCOX

Jawad Williams walks up to other friends with a broad smile on his face. They are not used to this. They worry that something is wrong.

"Why are you smiling?" they ask.

"I'm just happy," he says.

Jawad Williams and his brothers—he does not call Manuel and Scott teammates; he calls them *brothers*—have been through 8–20. And now they have been a part of the second-greatest comeback in the history of the Duke-Carolina rivalry. A few minutes before the game ended, it seemed impossible.

The seniors take the microphone at center court and address the crowd.

An emotional Manuel presents his parents with a rose, J. Williams addresses the crowd, Scott has some fun during his senior speech, and May and Terry share the court with jubilant fans (opposite, clockwise from top left); a record crowd of 22,125 people cheered on the Tar Heels (above).

Manuel brings tears to Roy Williams's eyes when he says, "I'd like to thank the coaching staff for helping me find myself."

Later, assistant coach Joe Holladay leaves the locker room and sees a friend. He smiles and shakes his head slowly. There is only one thing to say.

"Can you believe that?"

J. Williams is introduced as a starter for the final time at the Smith Center (opposite); Scott clips a piece of the net (right); the team takes a bow (below).

JIM BOUNDS

PEYTON WILLIAMS

73

Letdown in D.C.

CHAPTER THIRTEEN

Senior Day is a success.

The nets are cut. The ACC regular-season championship belongs to the Tar Heels.

Five days later Carolina has to play Clemson in Washington, D.C., in the quarterfinals of the conference tournament. The Heels have two wins over the Tigers already, a 19-point victory at Littlejohn Coliseum and a 32-point romp in the Smith Center. For almost a year UNC has been moving toward the NCAA Tournament, toward the three-week event that the players and coaches know will determine much of the way they are remembered.

But first there is this other event. Roy Williams is not a huge fan of the ACC's postseason gathering. But the coach tries to squash any ambivalence about the ACC Tournament immediately after the Duke game: "Guys, we're going to play in it. So we might as well win it."

The problem is this: Carolina has nothing to prove in Washington. The Tar Heels are assured of a number-one national seed and an NCAA placement in Charlotte for the first two rounds. Playing deep into the weekend will not earn them anything other than extra opportunities for injuries. All along they have

Coach Williams directs his team during the ACC Tournament game against Clemson (Mar. 11, opposite); Felton scored a career-high 29 points vs. the Tigers (right).

ROBERT CRAWFORD

75

thought
for the day

"Wasted potential is
the heaviest burden
in the world."

—*March 10, 2005*

ROBERT CRAWFORD

emphasized the importance of the regular-season crown, of surviving three months of conference play as the best team in the best conference in America.

The ACC Tournament rewards the best team over three days rather than three months. It is apparent soon after the Tar Heels arrive in Washington that they will not be that team. Blissfully straightforward freshman Marvin Williams turns to his head coach and says, "Coach, why do we play all of those games and then turn around and do it again? Why do three or four days mean as much as all the games we just played?"

"We all had the same idea: 'What's the point of this?'" Sean May says. "Anytime you step on the floor you want to compete. But we didn't have that bump in our step we normally have. Everybody was going through the motions, our defense was terrible, and it looked like our sophomore year. I had no motivation to play in the ACC Tournament."

It shows. Clemson shoots 61.5 percent from the field in the first half against the lethargic Carolina defense. Despite the return of Rashad McCants, who is in the lineup for the first time since the home win over the Tigers almost three weeks before, Clemson builds a 13-point lead with nine minutes remaining. Then Raymond Felton decides he is unwilling to lose. He scores the final 10 Tar Heel points, including a dramatic three-pointer that gives the Heels an 80–79 lead on the way to an 88–81 victory. The win saves Carolina from an embarrassing evening, as Roy Williams had promised to take the bus to Chapel Hill for a midnight practice if the Tigers pulled an upset.

Reserve Jesse Holley goes to the chalkboard in the locker room after the game and writes a pointed message to his teammates: "Hard work beats talent when talent doesn't work hard."

The Heels keep this in mind as they prepare for a semifinal matchup with Georgia Tech, a team they throttled by 22 points at the Smith Center in January. But the results are dismal. Will Bynum shreds the Tar Heel defense for 35 points, the Jackets take a 78–75 victory, and the salvage work begins.

Carolina's defense *was* bad, forcing Roy Williams to play as much point zone as he's used all year, but the offense was equally disturbing. The Heels mustered just 9 assists as a team. Jawad Williams sits in front of his locker, shoes off, pondering the defeat. Someone tells him the assists number.

He sits up, raises his eyebrows. "How many?" he asks.

"Nine."

A pained look crosses his face. "I didn't know that," he says. "Nine assists is something Ray can usually get by himself in a game or maybe even in a half. We didn't do a good job today of moving the ball and executing our plays, and it shows in that stat."

"It felt like we didn't want to be there," Melvin Scott says. "We just wanted to rest. We just weren't ready to play."

The team spends Saturday night in Washington before returning home Sunday morning. That evening, they gather at their head coach's home to watch the NCAA Tournament selection show. The year before Williams was perplexed by the squad's blasé reaction to being picked for the Tournament after a two-year hiatus. There was little excitement, little electricity, when "North Carolina" appeared on the screen. The players seemed almost bored.

There is no raucous cheering this year when the Tar Heels are slotted as the top seed in the Syracuse region. But Williams thinks he feels something in the silence—a businesslike determination.

The excitement is back. And so, after a weekend's absence, are the Tar Heels.

BOB DONNAN

May made 8 of 13 shots and had 3 blocks, but his teammates shot only 29 percent in the loss to Georgia Tech (Mar. 12, opposite); McCants returned after a four-game absence and scored 30 points in the ACC Tourney (above).

The Spark Returns

Five minutes and 33 seconds remain when Marvin Williams puts his body at risk and the season in peril.

Carolina leads upstart Oakland by 34 points, and the ball trickles loose near the baseline in front of the Tar Heel bench. It does not especially matter that it will be Oakland's ball. The Golden Grizzlies are overmatched, Carolina is cruising, and the NCAA Tournament's second round beckons.

Williams does not seem to care. He sees only a loose ball—*his* loose ball. Somewhere in the back of his mind, he probably hears the voice of his head coach breaking down the loss to Georgia Tech. The Tar Heels spent two and a half hours watching video of the first half of the game against the Jackets. One hundred and fifty minutes of film for a 20-minute half. Players alternately termed it "embarrassing" and "eye-opening."

"When you're out there on the floor, you don't see all those mistakes you're making," David Noel says. "Small things determine the outcome of the game and we didn't do those things at all. It was terrible

M. Williams scored 20 points against Oakland in the first round of the NCAA Tournament (Mar. 18, opposite); In the second round Carolina scored 92 points on Iowa State, including this dunk by Holley (Mar. 20, right).

thought for the day

"The bumps are what you climb up the mountain on."

—*March 16, 2005*

J. Williams meets with the media in Charlotte (above); Manuel soars for a basket (right). The Tar Heels shot 73.3 percent from the floor in the first half against Oakland.

watching it, and Coach kept rewinding it and rewinding it. That put something in our heads."

That something is still in the head of Marvin Williams as he lifts off in pursuit of the ball. He soars over two rows of photographers in a headlong dive as mouths drop open on the Carolina bench. This is the super-sub, the possible national freshman of the year, trying to clear a fair number of people and a lot of bulky camera equipment. This is dangerous. This is . . . well, Marvin.

"It scared me a little bit," Sean May says. "But that's the fearless passion Marvin has. That passion is what we needed. He brings that spark, and the spark had been missing."

The spark is not unusual for Williams. He is unfailingly polite off the court—members of the basketball support staff finally had to instruct him not to call them "sir" every time he addressed them—and unfailingly relentless on it.

"That's just me playing basketball," Williams says. "I was able to get to the ball, so I did it. Everybody was working hard. We all worked hard."

Williams is the latest in a long line of youngsters who grew up hoping to be a Tar Heel. His hometown is listed as Bremerton, Washington, but his family has deep roots in North Carolina, and he grew up watching his father's treasured series of Dean Smith instructional videos.

On Williams's official recruiting visit to Chapel Hill, his father and grandfather stopped by Dean Smith's office on the lower level of the arena.

The elder Williams said he could name the hometown of any Carolina player. "Go ahead," he challenged the former Tar Heel head coach. "Test me."

"Dick Grubar," Smith said.

The reply was quick and confident: "Schenectady, New York."

Smith's policy with freshmen was simple: no questions on the practice

court. The head coach believed freshmen were more likely to try to earn a quick rest by asking a question, so first-year players had to save their queries for later. There is no such rule under Roy Williams, and Marvin Williams has been one of the most frequent questioners throughout the season. At one juncture, Smith mentions his former policy to Roy Williams.

"It wouldn't work for Marvin," the current coach says. "He really wants to know the answer. He's not trying to get a rest."

He deserves a rest after his performance in Charlotte. Marvin scores 20 points and grabs 8 rebounds in 23 minutes against Oakland, then improves to 20 points and 15 rebounds (tallying a 12–10 double-double in the first half alone) in 26 minutes against Iowa State in the second round.

His teammates give him plenty of help, including a back-breaking three-pointer by Raymond Felton before halftime in the latter contest. Before the game, the Cyclones had expressed a desire to try and run with the Tar Heels. They get their wish, as Carolina uses a fast-breaking 19–2 blitz to seal the game early in the second half. Iowa State utilizes just six players; Carolina uses nine in the first half.

One of them is Marvin Williams, the quiet sub who has come off the bench in every game this year. "He is probably our most complete player," his head coach says.

And most completely unbelievable. After hurdling over photographers in the Oakland game, the freshman carefully retreats and prepares to return to action. But not before turning back to the photographers. Is he going to pull a Rodman? Will he blame them for being too close to the court? He opens his mouth.

"Hey, are you guys OK?" he asks.

M. Williams scored 20 points and grabbed 15 rebounds vs. Iowa State (left); Felton had 8 assists and 0 turnovers in the win over the Cyclones (opposite).

Two Steps to St. Louis

CHAPTER FIFTEEN

The Carrier Dome in Syracuse is an engineering marvel.

Sixteen 5-foot fans keep the 220-ton roof inflated. Visitors must obey airlock procedures on entry and exit to ensure that the roof remains propped open by the whooshing air.

The Tar Heels are inside the airlock when Steve Robinson nudges Sean May. "Hey, Sean," he says, "I've done my part."

May peers inside a plastic bag that the Carolina assistant coach holds and sees a 2003 Kansas Jayhawks Final Four T-shirt.

Robinson wears it to practice on occasion, usually to needle his players. When he donned it for the Wisconsin pregame shootaround, May had finally had enough: "Bring it to the game tonight and I'll rip it up," he told the coach.

"Only if you take care of your end and we win the game," Robinson responds.

May and M. Williams get excited during the Wisconsin game (Mar. 27, opposite); Coach Williams addresses his team during a timeout against Villanova (Mar. 25, above).

May's ever-present iPod earphones are humming as the team waits to enter the Carrier Dome. He did not sleep the night before. His roommate, Wes Miller, woke up in the middle of the night and noticed a very large human pacing the floor of the duo's hotel room.

"I asked him what he was doing," Miller remembers, "and he just mumbled something. I went right back to sleep, and he kept walking."

The tension vanishes when May sees the shirt inside the bag. He cracks a grin. The airlock doors release, and the team is ushered inside the building. He turns to Robinson.

"I'll see you after the game."

The season has been a challenge for Melvin Scott.

But the Carolina senior is used to challenges. He grew up in a rough section of Baltimore, in a neighborhood where drugs were prevalent. He was in and out of trouble as a child and found himself expelled from three different schools. His own mother threatened to banish him: "I can't have you in my house if you're going to act that way," she said.

Basketball rescued him. During high school Scott woke at 5:30 A.M. so that he could work out on the court before class started. His reputation grew. Gang leaders told their followers, "Leave the Scott kid alone." He still saw the gangs and the drugs, but he avoided their tentacles.

So two free throws are not that big of an issue. The score is Carolina 64, Villanova 62, and there are 28.9 seconds left in this third-round tournament game. Just a few minutes ago, the Tar Heel margin was 8 points and a ticket to the final eight seemed imminent. Now the Wildcats are roaring, Raymond

J. D. LYON JR.

Scott played the point for crucial minutes vs. Villanova (opposite); M. Williams scored 16 points, including 6 from beyond the arc (above).

Felton has fouled out, and a 74 percent free throw shooter is walking to the line.

It has been a roller-coaster first appearance in the Sweet 16 for these Tar Heels. Villanova runs an unorthodox offense relying on one-on-one matchups. They slice the Heels apart in the first 20 minutes. But Carolina's half-time routine is unvarying, even under these circumstances: For five minutes, the players are left to themselves. Some get medical treatments, while others change jerseys. The locker room is loud, with lots of voices shouting at once: "Somebody guard them!" "We've got to guard."

Meanwhile, the coaches meet in a separate room. Their conclusion mirrors the players' thoughts: The defense is terrible. Roy Williams enters the locker room, reprimands his team, and sends them back onto the Carrier Dome floor.

Now Melvin Scott stands two free throws from icing the game. Jawad Williams sits on the bench, his hands clasped in prayer. Strangely, he is not nervous. He leans over to Felton; they are two players who can do nothing but watch.

"Don't worry," Williams says. "He's going to knock them down. Melvin's going to make them."

Scott and Williams know almost everything about each other after spending endless hours shooting baskets in the Smith Center over the past four years. Williams's revelation comes when he sees Scott crack a smile. He knows what the smile means, knows that Scott is relaxed and that the shots are going in.

They do. The charity tosses earn Carolina a date with Wisconsin in the regional final.

When the Heels gathered at their head coach's house to watch the NCAA Tournament selection show, Roy Williams allowed himself a few brief thoughts about the Syracuse bracket. "I was shocked that Kansas was in our bracket," he says. "On a personal level, I didn't

JIM HAWKINS

May delivered 29 points and 12 boards vs. Wisconsin; Manuel scores 2 of Carolina's 44 second-half points against the Badgers (right).

J. D. LYON JR.

Felton accounted for 17 points and 7 assists in the Elite Eight (above); Wisconsin forward Zach Morley challenges M. Williams (opposite). The Tar Heels shot 53 percent from the floor against defensive-minded Wisconsin.

want that. I was shocked that Connecticut was in our bracket because in the old days, the committee would try to stay away from rematches, and we had already beaten them. I was shocked that we were going to have to play Connecticut in the Northeast, in Big East territory. So I was shocked about a lot of things."

As is usually the case in the tournament, upsets happen. Neither Kansas nor Connecticut makes it to the regional finals; the Jayhawks lose to Bucknell in the first round, and NC State drops the Huskies. So Carolina's road to the Final Four runs through the University of Wisconsin.

Roy Williams is not a fan favorite in Badger country. Wisconsin played a stultifying national semifinal against Michigan State in 2000, a game that was 19–17 at the end of the first half. After Kansas raced to a 99–98 victory over UCLA on November 9, 2000, Williams said, "Are you going to tell me you didn't like that more than 19–17 at halftime?" Although Williams and former Badger coach Dick Bennett have a very respectful relationship—Williams is fond of saying that, if he had to pick another style to coach, he would choose Wisconsin's—his Kansas team was loudly booed when they played at Madison in the 2002 NCAA Tournament.

Once again Williams again has an up-tempo, racehorse squad, and once again, Wisconsin will try to pour molasses on the tempo.

That's the pregame wisdom. But then the Badgers, who have scored more than 77 points only twice all season, keep up. At halftime the game is tied at 44. Wisconsin shoots 49 percent for the game and commits just 12 turnovers. Carolina exhibits the kind of lackadaisical defensive effort—excluding a timely block by Rashad McCants, who rejects a Clayton Hanson three-pointer with two minutes remaining—that Roy Williams has feared all tournament.

His team slips by with an 88–82 victory. It is a happy moment. Hugs are

exchanged, nets are cut, Final Four T-shirts are distributed. Another T-shirt doesn't survive the carnage. Sean May hunts down Steve Robinson and holds out his hands, palms up, for the offending Kansas item. Robinson delivers and May shreds it, to the delight of his teammates, in the middle of the locker room.

Roy Williams lets his team celebrate for a few minutes. Then he delivers the harsh truth.

"If you play defense in St. Louis the way you played it here, we'll be coming home after the semifinals," he says.

Final Four week has begun.

May and J. Williams embrace after earning a trip to the Final Four (opposite); Coach Williams clips the net (above) and then celebrates (with Felton, below) his fifth NCAA regional championship in 17 years as a head coach.

The Pit

I pledge to my teammates and my coaches, that I will give 100% mentally and physically on every defensive possession these next 7 days. I cannot imagine letting my teammates down on this nor can I imagine the hurt I will cause myself.

CHAPTER SIXTEEN

The practice plan is mysterious.

On the Monday after Carolina's regional final win over Wisconsin, the usual elements of the plan are in place: the Blue team, the White team, the offensive and defensive emphasis, the thought for the day.

But there is a 35-minute segment that's perplexing. It reads simply, "The Pit." Players see it as they prepare for practice and look quizzically at each other. The Pit?

Within the sanctuary of the locker room, there is another new addition. By the time the first player arrives to dress for practice, someone has used blue marker to write a simple paragraph on the board:

I pledge to my teammates and my coaches that I will give 100% mentally and physically on every defensive possession these next 7 days. I cannot imagine letting my teammates down on this nor can I imagine the hurt I will cause myself.

Felton's eyes reveal Carolina's defensive intensity vs. Michigan State (Apr. 2, opposite); Coach Williams urges his team to "compete" against the Spartans (right); the opening tip-off (pages 96–97).

thought
for the day

"Be led by your
dreams."

—March 30, 2005

Seventeen lines are drawn beneath the paragraph. By the time practice begins, the board bears 17 player signatures.

The Tar Heels go through their usual prepractice shooting drills, their warm-up fast-break drills. Then the routine changes.

"Now, then . . ." Roy Williams says, his usual indication that a new practice period is about to begin. "Let's go to The Pit."

He sprints through the visitor's tunnel of the Smith Center in the direction of the team's practice gym. Players, coaches, and managers follow him. It's the managers' duty to prepare every detail of practice, right down to the chewing gum that sits on a table for every coach. But Williams didn't tell the managers about The Pit. When the team gets to the gym, the lights are off and the door is locked.

"I'm turning around, and I'm ready to kill somebody," Williams says. "Here I am, I'm ready to run through the dadgum door, and it's locked."

The head coach turns to assistant Joe Holladay. "Did you unlock it?"

The answer is obvious.

Eventually, the door is opened. As they enter the practice gym, the players notice something ominous: The rims have been removed from the backboards. The next 35 minutes are focused entirely on the squad's usual defensive stations. No shooting. No dribbling. Just defense.

At the conclusion of the drill, Williams faces his team. "That was pretty hard, wasn't it?"

They respond in the affirmative.

"It's going to be harder tomorrow," he says. "We're going to be better defensively in St. Louis."

Four hours before their game against Michigan State, the Tar Heels gather for a pregame meal.

Coaches always try to gauge the intensity of their players at moments like this, to see how they're responding

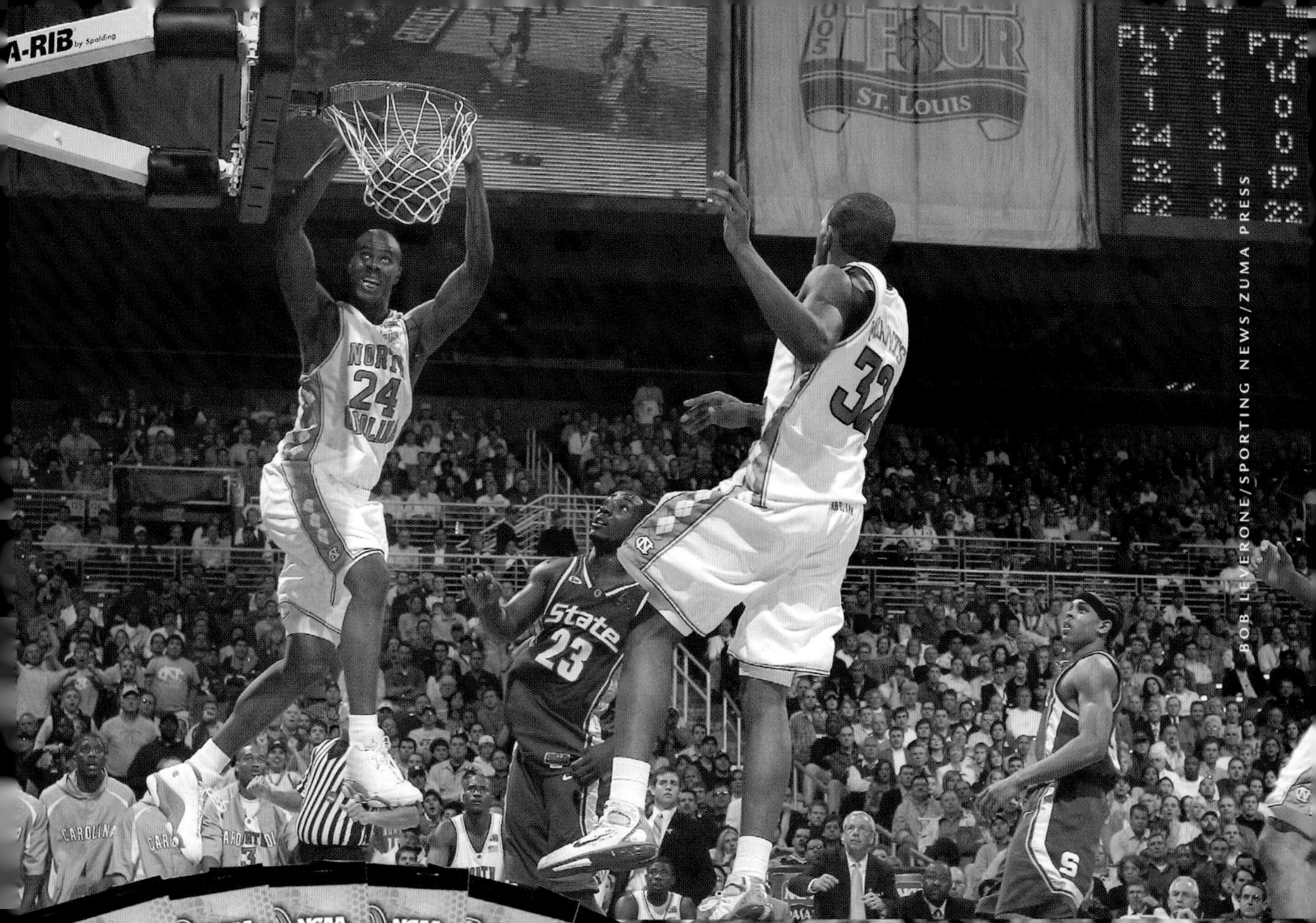

BOB LEVERONE/SPORTING NEWS/ZUMA PRESS

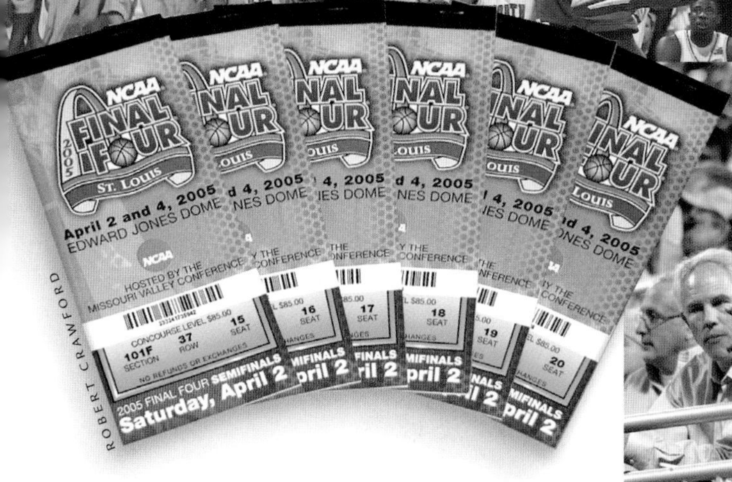

ROBERT CRAWFORD

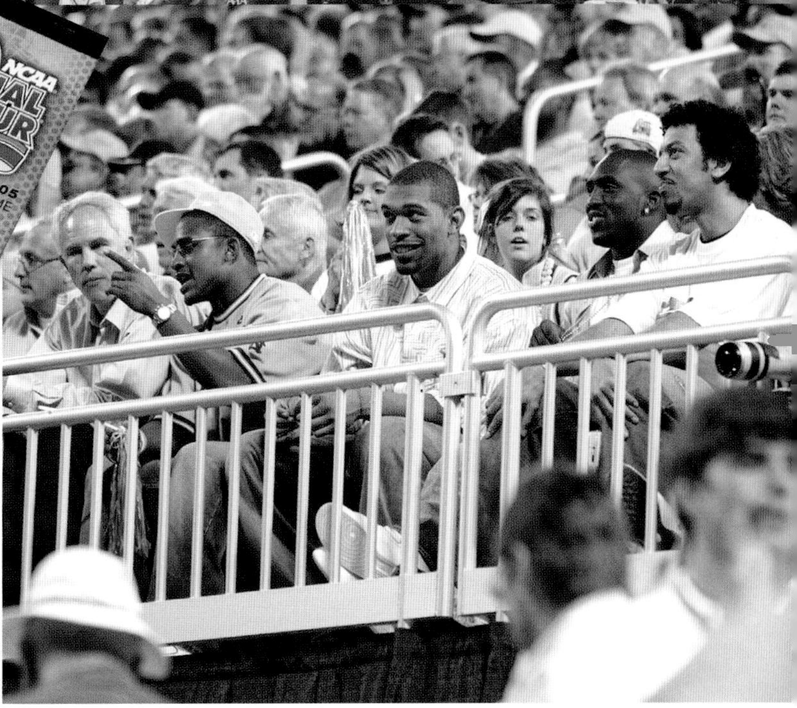

J. Williams scored 20 points against the Spartans (opposite); M. Williams puts an exclamation point on Carolina's semifinal win (above); Tar Heel alumni Mitch Kupchak, Dre' Bly, Julius Peppers, and Jason Capel cheered on UNC in St. Louis (right).

ROBERT CRAWFORD

to the pressure. The coaches are rarely successful, as there's virtually no way to predict how a team will play in a big game.

It is quiet in the hotel ballroom, but not because of nerves. The coaches have photocopied a newspaper article and passed a copy to each player on the roster. The article is not flattering. It is one of many that, in the week before the national semifinals, extol the virtues of Michigan State's teamwork, of their gritty approach to the game of basketball. The not-so-subtle implication is that Carolina is the complete opposite: a group of individuals content to use raw talent to bludgeon opponents into submission. The Tar Heels are slapped with a label and given the back-handed compliment of "most talented team." Talent, it seems, is something that requires an apology.

The sniping at their chemistry has an inverse effect. Every new article is met with more laughter. The team attends a banquet for Final Four teams in St. Louis and spends most of the evening looking like tourists, with video cameras rolling. They can't help but notice that the other teams seem to be having less fun.

Roy Williams looks out his hotel room window on the day before the game and spots vacationers cavorting under the Gateway Arch, throwing a football. Then he does a dou-ble take. They are not vacationers—they are his players.

Williams writes three points of emphasis on the locker room board before every game. It's his last chance to impart some strategic wisdom to his players. But one of the points on the board before Michigan State has nothing to do with Xs and Os. It just says "Have fun."

The first half is not fun. The Spartans build a 38–33 lead; Jawad Williams's 12 points are the only thing that keep the Tar Heels close.

Noel had 4 rebounds, 2 steals, and a thunderous dunk in the semifinals (above); Felton posted 16 points, 8 boards, and 7 assists (left); J. Williams made 9 of 13 shots from the floor (opposite).

JEFFREY A. CAMARATI

The senior, playing his best game in more than a month, boots his team into gear in the second half. He soars—on a tender hip—to slam through an alley-oop from Raymond Felton. He nails a fall-away jumper, a shot even he will later admit was not a good one, to give the Heels the lead. The rout is on, and lessons from The Pit are paying off. MSU makes just 33.8 percent of its shots in the second half.

Carolina has made a season-long habit of engaging in a locker room mosh pit after big wins. It's a bouncing, arm-waving, circle of emotion that even the coaches seem to enjoy. Roy Williams faces his team with one more game left.

"Guys, we can do that jump around thing and it will feel really good," he says. "Or we could wait until Monday."

They wait.

May scored 18 of his 22 points in the second half (opposite); J. Williams's 20-point performance earned him a postgame interview with CBS announcers Jim Nantz and Billy Packer (above).

National Champions

It is the night before the national championship game, and every player on Carolina's team has gone out to a party.

Well, not *out,* exactly. Just out of their rooms to the elevator lobby on the 14th floor of the team's downtown hotel. It's a surprise birthday party for Sean May, who turns 21 on April 4, game day.

"I love things like that," Roy Williams says. "Sean's mother, Debbie, had been concerned that it would be a distraction. But I thought it would be good for everyone."

It is good. The Tar Heels have 24 hours to endure before they can play the basketball game most of them have been waiting for all their lives. The hands of the clock do not move quickly.

10:00 P.M. Sunday: Jawad Williams walks over to the Gateway Arch. It is dark, and Williams is alone. The lines of

Felton drives on Illinois guard Dee Brown in the national championship game (Apr. 4, opposite); J. Williams grabbed 5 rebounds in the 75–70 Carolina victory (right).

105

thought
for the day

"To leave footprints
in the sands of time,
wear workboots."

—April 3, 2005

JEFFREY A. CAMARATI

McCants scored 6 of Carolina's 16 first-half field goals (above); M. Williams's dunk gave Carolina a 20–17 lead midway through the first half (opposite).

tourists that usually surround the monument are gone. "I wanted to be by myself," Williams says. "I took a couple of pictures and talked to myself, thought about how far I had come and about the chance we had to do something very special."

4:00 A.M. Monday: May is wide awake. Normally a sound sleeper, he hasn't rested well during the Tournament. His last sleepless night came the evening before the Wisconsin game, which he finished with 29 points and 12 rebounds. A repeat performance would be welcome.

5:30 A.M.: Jawad Williams is dreaming the same thing over and over, each time with a different ending. His Tar Heels have just won the national championship. "But every time I'd wake up doing something different to celebrate," he says. "One time I ran and slid across the floor. One time I ran into the crowd. One time I ran into one of my team-mates."

7:30 A.M.: May finally falls back asleep.

9:00 A.M.: In the world of college basketball, where killing time in hotels is an art form, this qualifies as an early wake-up call. The team has been shooting around on game days throughout the NCAA Tournament; they continue the trend at the Edward Jones Dome before returning to the hotel for a quick brunch.

1:00 P.M.: The afternoon turns into torture. There are still almost eight hours before tip-off. Assistant coach Joe Holladay barricades himself in his hotel room with one more Illinois game tape, hoping to find one last edge that might make a difference. He has noticed that the Illini make their play calls by jersey number—for example, a call of "four" means that number four, Luther Head, will probably shoot the ball.

2:00 P.M.: Former Carolina coach Dean Smith is inside his hotel room, catching up on some of the correspondence and dictation he's brought with him from Chapel Hill. He speaks to Roy Williams on a couple of occasions during the day but, true to his personality, prefers not to intrude.

106

2:45 P.M.: Still wired from the night before, May is watching a DVD of his father's sensational performance in the 1976 NCAA final. The elder May, Scott, scored 26 points and grabbed 8 rebounds as the Hoosiers defeated Michigan for the national championship. A handful of players—Jackie Manuel, Jawad Williams, Reyshawn Terry—trickle through the room as May watches. None is able to sit still for more than a few moments at a time.

Rashad McCants is watching a different DVD. He pops in the basketball movie "Coach Carter," the inspirational story of a high school coach. "I was so amped about the game," McCants says. "I just wanted to play. I could have gone to a court anywhere around us at that moment and played."

3:15 P.M.: Melvin Scott reads his usual pregame scripture, Romans 5:1–5. Without any fanfare, faith has played a major role in the lives of Scott and fellow senior Jawad Williams this season. Both were baptized earlier in the year, and Williams has taken to carrying a Bible with him at all times. One part of Scott's selected passage: "We rejoice in our sufferings, because we know that suffering produces perseverance; perseverance, character; and character, hope. And hope does not disappoint us . . ."

Scott turns to David Noel. "We're going to win, man," he says. "We're going to win it all."

4:00 P.M.: Everyone gathers for a meal at the hotel. Roy Williams goes over the keys to the game identified by the coaching staff.

5:15 P.M.: Finally, the time is melting away. The head coach takes his customary pregame nap, as does Jawad Williams. Some players read scripture. It is quiet on the team's 14th-floor retreat. Downstairs, Carolina fans turn the lobby into a noisy sea of blue.

Felton maneuvers around an Illinois forward (above) and guards Deron Williams (left); J. Williams, McCants, and Scott eagerly anticipate the end of the game (opposite).

J. D. LYON JR.

Felton made a key steal, then sank a free throw with 9.9 seconds to play for Carolina's final point of the 2004–05 season.

7:00 P.M.: McCants is one of the first Tar Heels out of the locker room. He does his usual pregame shooting routine, culminating with 25-foot three-pointers. Each time one of them finds the net, the early-arriving Carolina crowd—vastly outnumbered by the sea of Illinois orange that has turned the Edward Jones Dome into a road venue for the Heels—roars.

8:00 P.M.: The 2005 North Carolina Tar Heels gather for pregame instruction for the last time. By now, they know the plan: Watch for the Illini guards to penetrate and pass rather than penetrate and shoot. Keep Roger Powell off the glass. Help Raymond Felton contain Dee Brown, the quicksilver Illinois point guard. Create foul trouble for Illinois; make their bench contribute.

His team knows all the details. So Roy Williams focuses on the big picture.

"Last year we had a reunion," he says, referencing the Lettermen's Reunion that drew hundreds of Tar Heel basketball alums back to Chapel Hill. "Four of the five starters from the 1957 championship team were at that reunion. . . . They're always remembered as a national championship team. And 47 or 48 years later, the relationships they have and the memories they have are some of the strongest things about them.

"You guys have a chance to have that same feeling. You guys can get this done tonight. Somebody has to win. Why not let it be us?"

The message is powerful, but Williams debated using it.

"I fought with myself about whether to bring it up," he says. "But I thought it was a way for them to be led by their dreams, not pushed by their problems."

Three hours later, the last strand of net is cut.

Brightly colored streamers cover the floor. The national championship trophy has been passed around the Tar Heel locker room and currently resides in the locker of Marvin Williams. "I don't know why they brought it to me, but I'm going to hold on to it for a little while," he says.

Roy Williams has shared a tearful hug with his wife, Wanda, and his children, Scott and Kimberly. All those Final Four nights past that ended in disappointment. All gone in one rush of blue.

Terry, Coach Williams, Scott, and other team members hoist the championship hardware.

The head coach has climbed the podium and watched *One Shining Moment* with his team, sharing a shout of delight when Noel's dunk against Michigan State flashes on the video board. "I had watched that [the highlights special] for so many years, and I had always wanted to watch it from the arena, from the floor, when it was about my team," Williams says. "It was a moment where I reached up to wipe a tear away because as a coach, that is the moment. That's what you dream about."

Williams has presented Dean Smith and Michael Jordan to his players in the locker room. "Along with Phil Ford, these two guys *are* Carolina basketball," he tells the team. "But you have your moment right now."

There is just one last question to ask, one last mystery to solve. Six months ago three seniors gathered in the Smith Center and predicted a championship. How did they know?

"How else could it have ended?" Jawad Williams asks. "We've been the lowest and now we're the highest. We're champions. And that's something no one can ever take away from us."

Roy Williams is on the floor of the eerily quiet Edward Jones Dome, taping an interview with ESPN.

Just 30 minutes ago, the court was a blizzard of noise, streamers, and basketball players running around merrily, looking for someone to hug.

Now all the fans are gone. The players are in the locker room. Some members of the media remain at their workstations, but their voices are swallowed by the cavernous dome. It looks like the fairgrounds after the fair picks up and leaves town.

Roy Williams is the third UNC coach to win an NCAA title (top); Williams celebrated with Dean Smith and Michael Jordan (middle); Final Four MVP May made 10 of 11 shots from the floor against the Illini (bottom and opposite).

Williams stands at one baseline with a camera crew. He waits, occasionally checking his watch. He knows that his players are showering and heading for the bus, which will deliver them to a raucous reception at the team hotel. He gets in touch with assistant Jerod Haase.

Roy Williams doesn't want to walk out of the Edward Jones Dome, into what is sure to be an adoring crowd, alone. He tells Haase to ask any remaining players to hang around the locker room and wait for their head coach.

They comply. He returns to the locker room, exchanges a few more hugs and high-fives. Then they walk out of the building into the St. Louis night.

J. Williams and Grant amidst the streamers (opposite); May speaks at a postgame press conference (right); team members relax with their trophy (below).

Saying Goodbye

CHAPTER EIGHTEEN

They are literally surrounded by the rewards of their championship season.

At Carolina's annual end-of-season basketball banquet, the podium on the floor of the Smith Center is flanked on both sides by national championship trophies.

It is the final goodbye for the senior class, and the tears flow freely. Jackie Manuel breaks first, as the 35-minute video review of Carolina's season stirs up his emotions.

Chapel Hill's famous Franklin Street minutes after the title game ended (opposite); more than 15,000 fans welcomed the team home on April 5 (below).

DAN SEARS/UNC

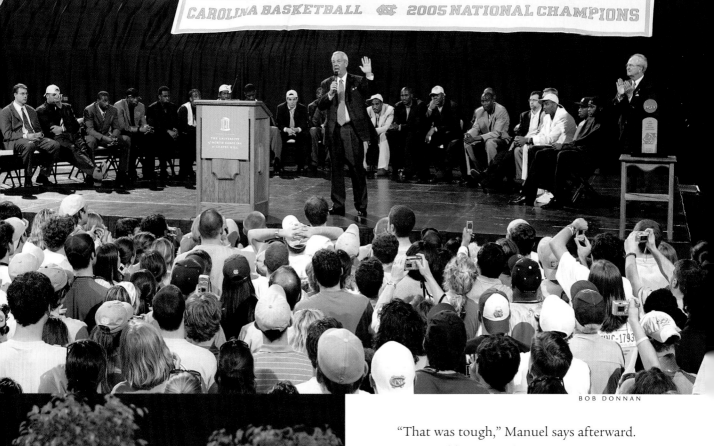

CAROLINA BASKETBALL NC 2005 NATIONAL CHAMPIONS

BOB DONNAN

JEFFREY A. CAMARATI

*Williams speaks at the celebration rally (top);
Scott delivers an emotional speech at the
end-of-year banquet (bottom).*

"That was tough," Manuel says afterward.
"It's emotional knowing that it's over. It really
hit me. That was the first time it hit me that
hard."

It looks like maybe it isn't going to hit
Melvin Scott. The designated jokester for the
Tar Heels wisecracks his way through the opening five minutes of his senior speech. No teammate is sacred, no coach left unzapped by his
quick wit.

But there has always been another side to
Scott, one he keeps hidden from all but his
closest friends. He tries to talk about his
mother. "Her strength and love . . ." he says, but
he cannot finish. He puts his head in his hands,
and the generous crowd of Tar Heel fans hushes
while his mother says, "Take your time, baby."

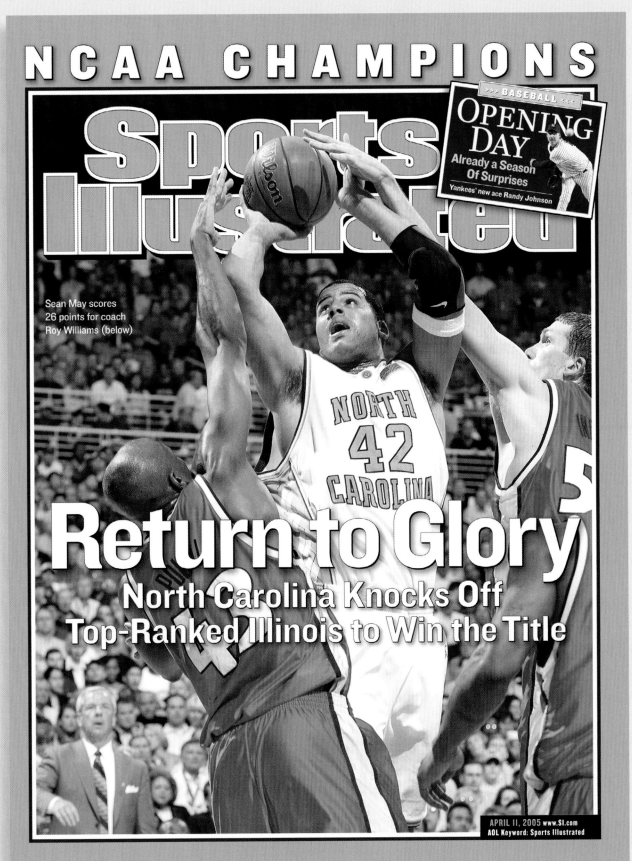

NCAA CHAMPIONS

Sports Illustrated

Sean May scores 26 points for coach Roy Williams (below)

NORTH 42 CAROLINA

Return to Glory

North Carolina Knocks Off Top-Ranked Illinois to Win the Title

APRIL 11, 2005 www.SI.com
AOL Keyword: Sports Illustrated

DAVID E. KLUTHO/SI

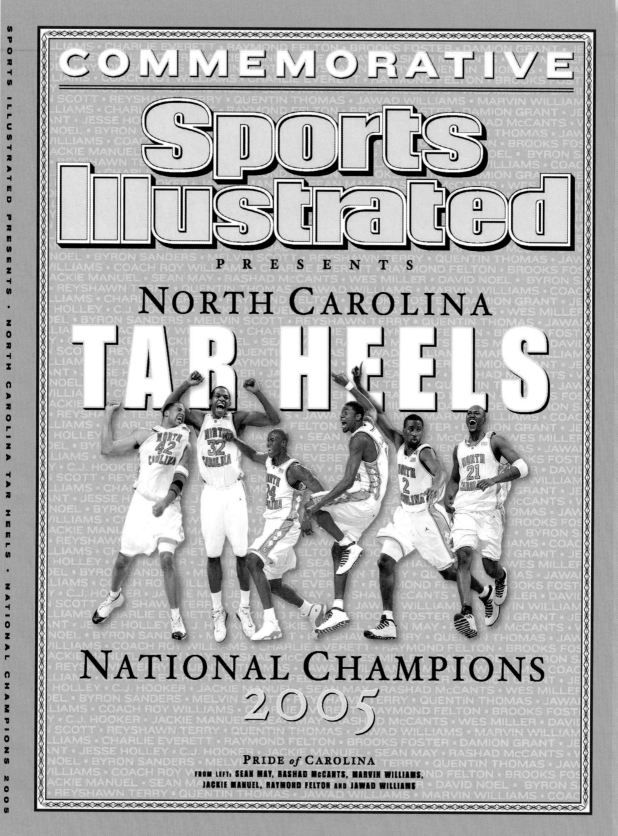

COMMEMORATIVE

Sports Illustrated

PRESENTS

NORTH CAROLINA

TAR HEELS

NATIONAL CHAMPIONS
2005

PRIDE of CAROLINA
FROM LEFT: SEAN MAY, RASHAD McCANTS, MARVIN WILLIAMS, JACKIE MANUEL, RAYMOND FELTON and JAWAD WILLIAMS

At the podium, where the team is sitting, there are 19 pairs of eyes locked on Scott—14 players and 5 coaches. Two pairs of eyes are not visible, because Jawad Williams and Manuel have their heads in their hands, too.

Jawad Williams goes last, and somehow that seems exactly right. He has been strong over the past four years. He was always the first one to put wins and losses in perspective, the first to dismiss any big game as "just another game."

Tuesday night, the realization that his college career has ended washes over him. He begins crying in the middle of Charlie Everett's speech and never really stops, an unusual outpouring of emotion from one so stoic.

"That's the first time it hit me since we won," Williams says. "It's over. I don't get to run out of this tunnel anymore. It was emotional, but I hope I was able to touch a lot of people."

Those people are Carolina fans and those people are Williams's teammates and coaches. They sit in the stands and on the podium, dabbing their eyes.

On the same Smith Center floor, Williams, Scott, and Manuel dreamed just six months before of capturing a championship.

"What if we did it?" Williams asked back then. "What if we finished this year with a national championship? From 8–20 to national champions. That would be something to write a book about. That would be a Carolina basketball story."

J. Williams and Manuel react to Scott's speech (above); Governor Mike Easley congratulated the Tar Heels at the executive mansion in Raleigh (right).

Roy Williams

The 2004 NCAA Tournament game against Texas was very disappointing.

It made me even hungrier to do better. We told each player that our team is going to be better because we've added some help. We're bringing in Quentin Thomas, we've got Marvin Williams, but the nucleus of the team is going to depend on what our returning players did. I challenged every one of them to do everything we asked in the areas they needed to improve. We did a nice job in the preseason conditioning program; that made me feel pretty good because we made it pretty strenuous. I was pretty tough on the kids.

I was dumbfounded when *Sports Illustrated* picked us No. 1 in the country. We weren't even picked to be number one in our league. People had such a high regard for Sean and Raymond and Rashad particularly; they sometimes didn't understand the holes those guys had in their game, so people were acting like the deficiencies were not there.

Coach Williams has taken five teams to the Final Four. He won his first national championship with Carolina in 2005.

123

> **Don't give me
> any excuses; it's
> time to produce.**

I was mad after the Santa Clara game, and I challenged them. We say we're going to do all this stuff, but the proof is in the pudding. We had an opportunity to step up and we didn't do it. So practice in Hawaii was going to be very constructive and very demanding.

The kids responded pretty well in Maui because I challenged them with the intensity of the drills and how demanding we were. There was no joking around, no casual comments. I said, "You had better be ready to work when you come in the door." I remember Rashad spraining his ankle and going off the court, and I didn't even walk over there. Marc Davis tied Rashad's shoe a little tighter, and Rashad came back on the court. It was at that point that I said, "Don't give me any excuses; it's time to produce."

Our intensity level was so much better in the BYU game. All of a sudden they saw what all could be accomplished when we were that intense on the defensive end of the floor and how good we could be when we started running up and down.

Raymond was embarrassed, he was mad, and he felt he had let his teammates down against Santa Clara. That made his intensity level even higher. I've never had to worry about Raymond's effort. I worry about some decisions, some missed shots or turnovers, but I've never had to worry about his effort. His focus was better against BYU, Tennessee, Iowa, than at any time his sophomore year. When he hurt his wrist, he just put it aside. All of a sudden everybody's saying, "That's a pretty good leader right there," and everybody fed off his toughness.

The win at Indiana helped us later in the year. We did not expect the kind of negative treatment Sean received, so we were even more determined to get this thing done. It was a very physical game—an ugly game at times—but we made enough shots, got enough stops. I told them, "This is going to be big for us the rest of the year." We took Indiana's best shot, and at the end of the game, we were able to make plays. The intensity we had was something I loved—and the toughness. That is something that came out more and more as our season went on.

Maryland and Georgia Tech were consecutive home games in January that would tell us a lot about our teams. I told them our goal should be to play great basketball and let the score take care of itself. If we did that, we'd handle people pretty easily at home. But when you're coaching, you try to put kids in a positive frame of mind, and I thought we could be really good if we focused on the defensive end of the floor, and if we rebounded the ball and got a running game going.

Maryland: We didn't get off to the best start, and they were making some shots. If we get the game going up and down the court, we're going to take their legs away—and then we can test their spirit. Are they going to give in, or are they going to keep going? That's what happened. We really got the tempo going, and then John Gilchrist got hurt, and there was nothing Maryland could do.

Georgia Tech: This is a big-time team that beat us in the 2004 ACC Tournament, and it left a bad taste in my mouth. So I challenged my team a little bit, saying "You had better be ready to play your A game." That was the first time I was impressed by our base—solid, fundamental defense. Kentucky, we'd made them turn it over; Indiana was an ugly game; but Georgia Tech was where I said, "We can guard people."

After the Wake Forest game, I pointed at specific players and said, "*You* as an individual did not play well; *you* as an individual did not play well; *you* as an

PEYTON WILLIAMS

individual did not play well. We can't have that. You've got to do your job to the best of your ability, whatever that job is. And if everybody does that, now we're playing as a team again. It's not individuals, it's our *team*."

In the first Duke game, the Blue Devils defense was so much stronger than our offense. They were so much more aggressive, and we were back on our heels. We're fumbling the ball and turning it over, and Raymond's having a tough night. Then some way, we got a little closer and we had a chance to win the game. I was really disgusted about the way we performed on the last play, but we competed and had a chance to win at the end, even though we had played so sorry. And I told them—I was not trying to con them—I was pleased about that part, that we had a chance to win that dadgum game at Cameron Indoor Stadium and we had played *poorly*.

Raymond was extremely disappointed in his play at Duke. The last play had gotten so much attention. So what I did is I picked out 10 or 15 plays, and I said, "All right, let's watch this. If you had done *this* differently, we may have won."

Picked out another play. "If you had done *this* differently, that would have saved us 2 points. It was a 1-point game, so we might have won." And I challenged the team to not let Raymond take the blame because everybody screwed it up. I gave instances where I screwed up. I said, "This is not on Raymond. Everybody understand that Raymond has to play better, and Raymond is going to play better, but don't let people blame this on Raymond Felton because Jawad, Sean, Rashad, Marvin, Roy—all you guys screwed it up. It was our team that lost the game." That was important, but the most important thing was that Raymond was so disappointed in his play that he just . . . *boom!* started making much better decisions and not taking so many chances with the ball.

Next we won a big road game at Connecticut. That game may have given our guys 10 times more confidence than the Duke game hurt their confidence, because we realized how good Connecticut was. I love going into somebody else's living room and stealing their brownies. It's just something I enjoy. I talk to the team about it all the time—nobody thinks we can win, but we know we can win.

With six games to go, I said, "We have a chance to control our own destiny. If you do what I ask you to do to the best of your ability for six games, you'll be conference champions. Don't worry about what Duke's doing. Don't worry about what Wake's doing. We are in control. If we play our tails off these three weeks, we're going to be the conference champions."

Two games later, we didn't have Rashad [who was suffering from an intestinal disorder]. We're going to play at NC State, and I said, "Against Santa Clara, I expected you to raise your level to make up for Raymond not being there. Now, I'm telling you we have to do this. You have to raise your level of play; you have to be able to come in and help this team." Again, they were so focused. Melvin Scott comes in and makes a bunch of threes, and every time State would make a little comeback, we would answer them. They scored 8 in a row, and we came down and scored 5 in a row. Their crowd's going crazy; and we come down and get a stop.

In the next game Raymond finished a big-time play, and

"I love going into somebody else's living room and stealing their brownies."

we won at Maryland. He was still holding on to the Duke game and the fact that he did not make a play when he had the opportunity, and I told him, "Now you did. So put that one behind you." That was important to Raymond—that he made a play when he had to make one.

In retrospect, Rashad's absence may actually have been a blessing because Melvin and David Noel did feel better about themselves and how important they could be. Reyshawn Terry did more things and came off the bench and gave us better moments. Those guys felt even better about themselves and had more confidence.

I offered the seniors the chance to cut the nets after the Florida State game. I said, "Now, all this guarantees us is a tie [for the regular-season championship], but you have earned the right if you want to cut them down." They said no, no, no. Jackie immediately said, "No, we've got one more game." I loved that because it made me feel they were going to really be focused for Duke.

Some of the most emotional days I've ever had in my career are Senior Days because I'm not going to get to coach those kids in our building anymore. With this group, Jawad and Jackie and Melvin, it was very emotional because of what they had gone through as freshmen and the way

PEYTON WILLIAMS

JEFFREY A. CAMARATI

they had continued to come back. They hadn't left; they didn't transfer—they came back to try to make the team better.

You can't lose your last home game—that's just not right. I get cold chills thinking about that final home game against Duke. With three and a half minutes to play, I said, "If you'll do exactly what we say and give me a total commitment on every possession—not to do well, but to do the best—then we're going to win this game." Jawad had his head down, and I flicked him on the head and said, "Get your head up. We're going to win this game, but it's got to be a total commitment. It can't be 'Okay coach, I'm going to do this.' You have to *do* it. You have to do it right now better than you have ever done it before."

Destiny. I believed we were going to win that game. I told David Noel, "Don't reach around behind and try to slap the ball away. That just takes you out of defensive position, and these guys are too good. You're not going to be able to stay in front of the guy." So during that comeback, what does he do? Daniel Ewing goes past him; David reaches around behind. There's a loose ball on the floor, and three guys are calling timeout. It is our possession. We shoot free throws; we miss the second one. Raymond, who

JIM BOUNDS

JEFFREY A. CAMARATI

is not supposed to go to the board, went to the board anyway and knocked it loose. Marvin picks up the ball and scores. Maybe it was destiny. But I tell you what, I believed we were going to win that game.

For Sean to go 26 points and 24 rebounds was mind-boggling. I got the stat sheet in the locker room and said, "Sean May, you were really something today." I do believe that gave that youngster even more confidence. With each and every game, he started playing better and better, and we started depending on him more. Without Rashad, Sean became even more of a threat offensively. It was crucial to get the ball inside and for him to deliver. The Duke game gave him a lot of confidence because this is Duke, this is Shelden Williams, who through the first half of the year may have been the best player in the ACC.

J. J. Redick had 17 points in the first half, but I think he only took four shots in the second half. His teammates didn't forget him; they would still look for him, but Jackie made him unavailable. Redick was not an option.

There were times during the year when somebody would say, "We just gotta get a break. We gotta have an offensive rebound. We gotta get a steal." As soon as it would be said, Jackie would do that. He gave up his feelings and his attitude to help this team. He did it last year, and he did it again this year. At Connecticut, he was sick as a dog, throwing up in a towel, and I put him back in, and the first play he came up with a steal. In the Duke game he was getting to the offensive boards. In the NCAA Tournament, he was chasing the other team's best shooter and best scorer every time—and doing it for a coach who, when he got here, told him, "I can't have you shoot the ball anymore." I'll remember so many things about the 2005 team, but the sacrifices Jackie Manuel made and the kind of person he is, and—I'm not ashamed to say it—the love I have for him, those are good moments.

The ACC Tournament turned out to be a letdown for us, and I was afraid it was going to happen, but it was my fault. I challenged them with three weeks to go in the regular season. After the emotional win against Duke—winning the conference championship and celebrating and just feeling so good about what we had done—we thought, "Now we have to play them again?" I completely believe our poor play in the ACC Tournament was because I emphasized those last six games so much. And if I had to do it over again, I'd do the *same* blessed thing. You don't have many chances to win an outright regular-season conference championship, and I wanted that for those kids.

They refocused so quickly—it was amazing. After Santa Clara I told them that twice as a staff at Kansas, we had lost the first game of the season and both times we had gone to the Final Four. I told them we had gone to the Final Four four times, and we had never won the conference tournament. People remembered those Final Four teams. They didn't remember near as fondly '97, '98, '99, when we had won three straight conference tournaments. We talked about that, and we talked about getting focused to play our best basketball for three weeks.

I've had a couple of teams that have gone to the NCAA Tournament and been very tight. The stress had gotten to them. They wanted to please people so much that it hurt their play. I didn't want us to be tight; I didn't want us to feel any pressure. I wanted us to be able to focus and have fun. It was a concerted effort on my part to make sure we were loose.

Every aspect of our play was better in Charlotte than it was in the ACC Tournament. The players enjoyed being in the NCAA Tournament. They enjoyed staying longer than one game. They enjoyed the winning. I said, "Hey, this is pretty good, but you have no idea how much fun it can be—how much fun it's going to be—if you play. You've got memories that nothing will ever take the place of, but only if you really play."

Seeing the way we played Oakland and Iowa State, our coaching staff thought this tournament could be something special. Some teams, once they get into the tournament, just start building momentum from that first game. Play great and then play great again, and then keep it going.

There's no question I would rather have played Villanova when they had

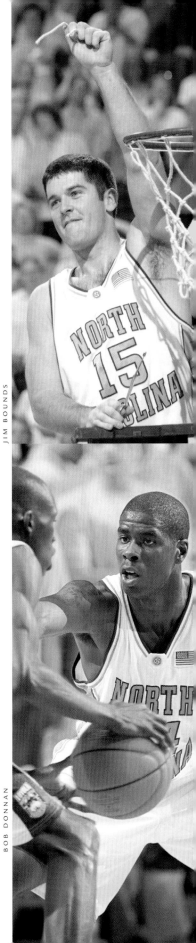

JIM BOUNDS

BOB DONNAN

131

> **I don't look at the scoreboard in the first half, even when we're getting whacked like that.**

two big guys because without those two players, it was a bad matchup for us. With Curtis Sumpter injured, they played four guards, so Marvin or Jawad had to go out on the floor and defend a guard. It was to Villanova's advantage. I don't look at the scoreboard in the first half, even when we're getting whacked like that. I may look at the scoreboard one time. But it's a 40-minute game, and I've always said that if you guard people, they're not going to make those shots for 40 minutes. We made a little run right before the half. I remember going in with the coaches and saying, "Gosh, we're really lucky we're not down even more than we are because we didn't play very well."

We played the last few minutes without Raymond, but it's not about one individual. At one of the timeouts I said, "We're okay. This group is good enough to win. You don't have Raymond, but this group is good enough to win."

We talked about how everybody has to help Melvin. Everybody come to meet the ball even more; everybody get to your spots quickly and sharply. And everybody picked that level up a little bit. We made a couple of shots. Melvin made some good decisions and some free throws. The one play everybody wants to talk about is the travel [called against Villanova's Allan Ray with about 10 seconds left in the game]—but even if the referee hadn't called that, they had to make the free throw to even tie the game. We had the lead. But I thought it was a walk.

Wisconsin had a player [Mike Wilkinson] who was very difficult to guard inside. We made some clips to show to our team, and we challenged Sean. Then his teammates got after him: "Boy, you're in trouble. I don't know that you can guard this guy." So Sean was more focused going into that game. And then early he realized, "I'm bigger. I'm stronger." There's no question we had to get the ball to him. Sean got positive feelings from Melvin and from Jackie, too. I mean, we gotta get the big dog the ball.

I had gotten really mad at Rashad in the first half over his offensive play, and I took him out. I can get mad at you, but then I move on. I'm not going to come back and belabor the point for an hour and still be thinking about that. I said,

"Now, you screwed it up. Put that behind you, and let's go play." And he made the big three [to put UNC ahead 81–75 with 1:09 to play], then blocked a shot. It is amazing because one big defensive play—if it's at the right time—is more important that a lot of them. Just one at the right time.

Rashad made some big-time sacrifices this year. His shot selection was better, and he took fewer shots. But he was able to do some big-time things to help us win, and he did it because he thought it was going to be best for the team. It was not ol' Roy doing this—Rashad made those sacrifices, and his teammates realized that and saw him sharing the ball and giving it up more instinctively.

I was skeptical about what kind of attitude the team would have about making it to the Final Four. When you leave on Monday night with the prize, that's the best. There's no one that can ever take that away from you. But you can't be just *satisfied* to be here, so we attacked with the same kind of plan. We wanted to make it the same as the first and second rounds, the same as the regionals, with one exception: We wanted to play better. That whole week we worked extremely hard on the defensive end of the floor. My whole attitude was, why not play our best basketball of the year this weekend? Why not play our best defense this weekend?

Before the Michigan State game, the practice plan included something called "The Pit." We got through the first shooting drills, a couple of fast-break drills, and I said, "All right, let's go to The Pit," which I'd never called it. But I said "Follow me," and I jogged into the practice gym. We had taken all the rims off the backboards. I said, "Fellas, for 35 minutes we're going to be in here, and we're going to be better in St. Louis than we were in Syracuse." For 35 minutes we did defensive stations and defensive drills with a tremendous amount of enthusiasm. I said, "All right, let's go back and finish practice." The next day we did the same thing. After that, I said, "That's it. We're going to be better." That was important to our whole attitude.

One of the staff (I think it was Joe Holladay) said, "Give them the pledge again." A couple of years ago at Kansas, I was frustrated because our guys weren't boxing out, so Coach Smith said to have the players sign a pledge. We did it at Kansas, and it worked. So we did it again with this team on Monday after Syracuse. I wrote something like this up on the board: "I will not let my teammates down on the defensive end of the floor." I drew 17 lines underneath it. I went out on the court before practice started and said, "Hope everybody saw what I wrote up on the board." When practice was over I went into the locker room, and all 17 guys had signed that. They didn't know what those little lines were for or anything, but 17 guys had signed it. That was special.

JEFFREY A. CAMARATI

We didn't play well in the first half against Michigan State. I think in the Final Four some teams will be timid. They don't know about the hype and the pageantry; they haven't been there before. I got after our players a little bit at halftime, asking, "Why would you not box out?" We had a guy not box out and give up an easy basket. We had another guy turn sideways and not take a charge. I said, "Fellas, this is the Final Four. David, I'll take a charge on you with Damion on your back. This is the Final Four."

In the second half we began to run more consistently—run every time—and we did pick up our defensive play. We did stand in and box out. We did not back over and let somebody drive in and lay it up. So every aspect of our game picked up, and with each one of those different factors, we'd get a better shot or we'd get a fast break.

I was really proud of Jawad that night. He had been struggling quite a bit, but he kept focused and he was getting a little more healthy. His knee was bothering him, he was banged up a little bit, and the guy who was coming in for him—Marvin—was playing lights-out. But Jawad hung in there, and I told him, "I'm not giving up on you. I'm still running you out there. I still have confidence in you, so you should have confidence in yourself."

Getting ready for Illinois, all the talk in the media was "team versus talent." I was really mad because that's an insult to my staff, my team, and me. It was a slap in the face to our coaching staff, to what we'd worked on for 98 practices. I told the kids, "It should make you mad. I want it to make you mad. And I want to shut them up." Two-thirds or three-quarters of the crowd is going to be from Illinois anyway, and now these so-called experts are saying, "You're not a team." It really ripped me. To be honest with you, I saw it was making the players mad, and I liked that. I said, "Let's do some things and show them we're a team."

Illinois was going to run back at us, so we had to sprint back and get them picked up quickly because they could rush it up, could pull up and shoot threes; they could do those kind of things so quickly to score points. I said, "Let's take away their legs; let's run it back at them—make them play defense so hopefully at the end of the game their legs won't completely be there. Maybe they'll miss some of those shots at the end of the game." That was the number-one thing: Get picked up and get them stopped; get them under control a little bit and stop them from getting anything inside so they have to shoot the ball from the outside.

Illinois' post players are good, but they're not at the same level as their three first-team All–Big Ten guards. We had an advantage inside because we have Sean May, who's kicking everybody's rear, and we have Jawad and we have Marvin. We have to get the ball inside because if we do that, we're going to get their guys in foul trouble. We put on the locker room board: "The ball must go inside by dribble or pass."

In the first half we built a lead by attacking Illinois. There were three things: sprint back and get picked up, get the ball inside, and we must attack. We always say "attack under control" and "attack and make good decisions." We were in attacking mode. And we did get the ball inside.

Former Tar Heels George Karl and Doug Moe in St. Louis (below).

In the second half Illinois started making threes. There was one time I was a little concerned about the look on our players' faces. I said, "Hey, it makes no difference what they're doing. They're making all these shots. We're still going to control the game." At two different timeouts I said, "We're going to be fine." I was trying to give them some confidence and get them to understand that, hey, we're still in control. We're going to determine the outcome.

Raymond made a big shot with the score tied at 65. My first thought was that it was a tougher shot than he needed to take. Then the ball was no more than halfway there, and I said, "That's going in." I thought of the first game against Duke, when he didn't make a play at the end and got criticized so much for it. Here's a young man who's willing to make a play—and is capable of making a play.

Sean was sensational in the Final Four. You hear all the time, "That was the year Jack Givens did this, that Danny Manning did this." Now they are going to say "2005 was the year Sean May did this." I felt with his play down the stretch, he should have been the ACC Player of the Year. In the NCAA Tournament he was special in every game. Against Illinois, Jackie said, "Guys, let the big dog eat. Give the boy the ball." That's what Jackie said as they were coming over to the bench.

To hold teams like Michigan State and Illinois to under 30 percent in a half is incredible. Even down the stretch in the championship game, I said, "We're going to win it on the defensive end." As a coach, I take a great deal of pride in how we were much better the week after Syracuse. Those two games in St. Louis were maybe our two best defensive games of the year.

There's going to be times when we must stop the other team. You're either on the ball, you're one pass away and denying, or you're more than one pass away and in help position. We talked all year about doing it to the best of your ability. Raymond was where he was supposed to be, and Luther Head threw him the ball. We kept saying the last three minutes, "Come on guys, one more stop. We must stop. One more must-stop." We didn't call it just "stop." It was a *must-stop*. That attitude on the defensive end made Raymond be in the right spot.

I said, "If we win a national championship, I'm going to walk around with my arms up in the air." Later my son Scott said, "You forgot what you were supposed to do, didn't you?" The last shot is taken and Sean gets the rebound, and I look up and see the clock, and I look back at Sean and he's still got it, and I look back at the clock, and I see it go 0:00. To this day and the day I die, it was like a fog. I didn't know what to do. I didn't know how I was feeling.

C. B. McGrath grabbed me, and it was a great hug. Then he went away, and here comes Sean. A hundred million dollars I would give up before I would forget that memory—that big, smelly, sweaty rascal coming and hugging my neck, and saying how happy he was. Money can't buy that kind of feeling.

Sean said in a press conference that he had thoughts of being on the team that won me my first national championship, and it almost got me. I tried to pinch my knee or something. I didn't feel like I could lose it up there. I thought, "Here's a youngster that has a chance to be on basketball's biggest stage, and he wants to win one, not just for Roy Williams, but he wanted to be on *that* team." When he came over and hugged me on that sideline, and the way he made me feel at that moment—you can't match that.

I really don't think I am a better coach than I was before that game started. The way people would say things about "can't win the big one" bothered my family more than it did

"Here comes Sean. A hundred million dollars I would give up before I would forget that memory—that big, smelly, sweaty rascal coming and hugging my neck . . ."

BOB LEVERONE/SPORTING NEWS/ZUMA PRESS

me. They had been there when we had lost those games. I asked [Athletic Director] Dick Baddour to see if Wanda [Williams's wife] would come down on the court, but Dick said, "She's not coming down there." So I went over to the stands and I hugged her, and she had tears in her eyes, and it was hard for me at that moment. Then I asked people in the crowd, "Can you get Scott? Can you get Kimberly?" They [Williams's kids] came down, and both of them were crying.

It was one of the greatest moments you can have, and yet you and your family are sitting there, and all four of you are crying. You know, it's one of those tears-of-joy kind of things—there's no question about that—and it was different than Sean's hug because Sean's hug was of joy and thanking me and, in his way, giving me the victory as a coach. Wanda and Scott and Kimberly had been through some . . . not tough times because we're talking about a game, but I'm pretty emotional, and things affect me for a long time. It was a feeling of relief.

I thought about my mom. In 1991 Kansas played North Carolina in the semifinals and won. She said she had always been proud of me, and she always thought I would do something that would continue to make her proud. She passed in 1992, and she had told Michael Jordan's mom and dad that the most fun she had ever had was at the Final Four in '91. So I did think of her. My dad passed away last May. He had only seen me coach two games in my entire life. Our relationship at the end had gotten a lot better, so I thought of him.

I kept looking over to the North Carolina section because so many people were there to watch North Carolina win a national championship. A lot of them were there to see me after it was over with. I'm very lucky because I had a lot of people who wanted me to get that monkey off my back. I kept looking at those people and saying, "I hope they know how much I appreciate them and love them"—our former players (George Karl, Doug Moe, Mickey Bell); Buddy Baldwin (my high school coach); my golfing buddies, and the whole bit. I kept pointing over there because I wanted our team to understand—let's thank those people there. And I tried to get them to show the trophy around. It was important for me to show that trophy to the North Carolina people because they are what make this place pretty special.

Back in the locker room, I grabbed Coach Smith and said, "Thank you." He's the one responsible for Roy Williams having these kinds of moments. It's not because of Roy Williams—it's because of what Coach Smith did for me, how he enabled me to be in that position. Then I turned, and there's Michael Jordan. He just picked me up in a big bear hug, picked me up off the floor. I said, "Thank you so much for being here." He said, "There is no way I was missing this, watching you win your national championship. There may be more to come, but there was no way I was going to miss this one." That was something. I got the team together and I pointed at Michael and Coach Smith, and I said, "This is North Carolina basketball. These guys and Phil Ford—*they* are what made North Carolina basketball. But now you are part of North Carolina basketball forever."

If there was one key moment this year, I strongly believe it was after the

Coach Williams with North Carolina Governor Mike Easley.

loss to Duke, when I challenged every player: "Don't you let people blame this loss on Raymond. It was my fault. It was Rashad's fault. Sean, it was your fault. Wes [Miller] and you guys that didn't play in the game, it was your fault. If you had worked harder in practice the day before . . . If you had prepared us better . . ." I went around the room and told everybody on our team, "It's not Raymond's fault, and don't you let him take that blame." They believed it, and Raymond appreciated it. From that moment on Raymond Felton was a different player, and from that moment on Raymond was willing to make big plays. And our players knew it wasn't about individuals, it was about *team.*

JEFFREY A. CAMARATI

Jerod Haase

Watching Coach Williams cut down the nets was a great moment.

Having been a player under him and having been on his staff now for six years, to see him cut down the nets and see the emotion after the game was really special to me.

His work ethic, his honesty, and his integrity make the players learn to trust him and play hard for him. You want to do everything for the guy. Over these two years the current players learned to respect him. You learn to play hard for him because of that respect, and you love him like he's a family member. Relationships are so important to Coach Williams, his coaching style, and his program. The longer he is around people, the stronger those relationships are, and the better he understands people he is working with and how to motivate them.

It was difficult this year for me to step back from the bench. I had one year as an assistant coach and wanted to be in the huddles, in the locker rooms in every situation, and be in the fire. I treated the whole year as a learning experience. It was good for me to watch Coach and predict the substitution patterns, when he was going to call a timeout—or predict when a play was going to be called. I wasn't always right, but understanding why he did those things is important to me.

Haase has played for or been on staff with Coach Williams since 1993.

There were points when I thought we had the character, the teamwork, and the energy to win the national championship.

Winning at Indiana, where we didn't play particularly well in a hostile road environment, was a huge stepping stone because it showed we could win in a tough environment. Beating Duke was a big stepping stone because it showed we could win a game against a really good team under adverse circumstances. Once we showed we could do that, the opportunities were endless.

Going into the season, Coach didn't make any big changes. Coach has a philosophy and a belief in how a system and a program should be run, some-

thing he learned from Coach Smith. So he doesn't believe in doing major overhauls. As his career has gone on, he has probably shortened practices a little bit more and put more trust in the players to take care of their conditioning and get their shots up. The team responded to that, and it helped with fresh legs throughout the season.

We learned a lot from the Santa Clara game. Coach was able to refocus the team and tell them, "We are still able to do some great things." Things were going along so well in the preseason—there really wasn't a stumbling block. The team was able to turn the Santa Clara loss into a stepping stone.

This team responded well to adversity all year. Coach Williams is a lot of things: He's a great coach, great person, great recruiter. He knows how to run a program. But above all else, he's a great teacher. After losses, he is able to teach the players why it was a loss and give them information about how the next one can be a win. Even more so than other times, the guys really pay attention, and Coach gives them the information they need to go ahead and win the next game. That's one of the reasons we were able to run off some impressive win streaks after each of the four losses.

If there was one player on this team I identified with the most, it would have to be Jackie Manuel.

Jackie was so instrumental to this team and did so many good things. He gave completely of himself when Coach came to Carolina. Jackie said, "If you want me to guard, I'll guard. If you want me to not shoot as many threes, I'm not going to shoot as many threes." His willingness, his enthusiasm for the game, his love of the university, his love of Coach Williams, and his love of his teammates really stood apart.

Winning the ACC regular-season championship was a tremendous accomplishment, something that had not been done here in 12 years. It was an important goal for Coach and the team. Anything in life—the more you put into it, the more you are going to get out of it, and the more you appreciate what you've done. The ACC championship is many games, many practices, many hours of blood, sweat, and tears. When you put that much work and energy in something, the reward at the end and the feelings you get are that much more important.

Coach did a great job of leading the team by example during the NCAA Tourna-

Haase with Mick Mixon and Woody Durham in Syracuse.

ment. He had been there before and the staff had been there before, but the players had not been to that elite level. They relied on Coach to show them how to be composed in those situations, and they followed his lead. He kept the players loose, but he made the point that if you want to win championships, you have to be good on the defensive end of the floor. Guys took that to heart.

Winning the championship reinforces everything Coach Williams teaches: If you do the right thing and work hard, progress will be made and good results will follow. I can't think of a more positive result than the one we achieved that Monday evening in St. Louis.

Joe Holladay

Adapted from videotaped interviews

I have the dubious pleasure of sitting by the players when they get taken out of the game, so I hear all the good stuff and the bad stuff.

Last year, our first as a staff at Carolina, sitting on the bench next to them was like being in purgatory. The players didn't like me when they came out, and I didn't like them because they always wanted to know *why* they came out.

What a change a year makes. This season they never asked, "Why did I come out?" Not one time. That's a pretty good sign of maturity.

It probably took a full year for the players and coaches to fully trust each other. When we first got here, the players never came back to our offices; they never got past the front desks. I don't think you can overemphasize that trust factor, building those relationships. Coach Williams did a good job this year convincing the players that he had faith we were going to make the play—somebody was going to hit a big shot. He really trusted them. He'd say, "You have North Carolina written across your uniform because you're a good player, or you wouldn't be here. Now go make plays. We'll put you in positions to do things, but then you go make the play."

JEFFREY A. CAMARATI

Holladay has been on Roy Williams's coaching staff since 1993.

ROBERT CRAWFORD

Our relationships with the players got better. They came by our offices more, or they closed the door to talk to us more. I really enjoyed these guys. Besides being good players, they've got a lot of personality. It was more of a man-to-man relationship this year with the players. They're college kids, and we're their coaches—but they still had respect, and you didn't have to worry about being on guard all the time. You could say what you wanted to.

Some of that trust developed in practices when Coach did something entirely different. The players think they're going to practice, then all of the sudden he says, "Well, if you sing to me, you don't have to practice." That's where the first version of the Singing Tar Heels came about. Little things like that help the bonding process between team and coaches. Coach started to give them some slack, laughing at things that a year ago might have been a little more serious.

When practice began in October, I felt better because I saw determination.

These guys came back focused, and the key component was buying into Coach Williams's system. You could tell when practice started because there were never any excuses.

Don't think for a second that the players hadn't heard for a long time how good they are. They finally wanted to do something about it: They wanted to put their talent into a team situation and win. This team had exceptional ability, but it also had some holes. We weren't the strongest defensive team all the time. We weren't the best ball-handling team. But we had a core that would bring it every night. And the Blue team brought it to our top eight every day in practice. They were tough, and that toughness caught on. We had kids that did not want to lose.

I wasn't worried when we lost to Santa Clara. I knew we had a dang good team, and we didn't have Raymond Felton in that game, who all of our guys counted on. I *was* really worried when Raymond hurt his wrist against Tennessee. I didn't mind him missing one game, but I was thinking, "We have to do whatever to protect this young man . . . if we have to put a cast on, if he doesn't have to ever practice again and just play the games—whatever." If anyone touched Raymond in practice, they were going to pay the price from me.

Maui was where I decided that this team was going to win the national championship. I know that's easy to say now, but my wife, Roi, will tell you,

"Joe said they were going to win the national championship all year long. He said they were going to win the whole thing."

Every time we had a loss, it was a timely loss.

It was a wake-up loss. It refocused us every time. At Wake Forest we got beat by 13, and we didn't play great, but we didn't play bad. We're pretty dang good if we go to the fourth-ranked team in the country and get beat by 13, and it's a close game, and they hit 32 out of 32 from the line. Nobody liked the loss, but down deep we had to get a little confidence from it.

At Duke everyone was mad because we didn't get a shot at the end. Everyone asked, "Why did it come down to the last shot?" We had too many turnovers; they had 17 steals. That has to be a national record against a Roy Williams team, and for us to have 23 turnovers . . . That refocused us again for the rest of the conference.

The players were nit-picking at each other during the Georgia Tech loss in the ACC Tournament, in my opinion, and that's the first time that had surfaced. They were defending themselves; they were getting on somebody else. Everything had been going well as we finished off the league, and then all of a sudden things weren't going right against Clemson. So it kind of surfaced right there, and it came to a head the next day when we got beat by Georgia Tech. We weren't as much of a team as we needed to be, but our guys were smart enough to realize that they were nit-picking at each other. That brought us back together, made us tighter because they realized they're not as good when they play as individuals.

I get emotional thinking about what this title means for Coach Williams.

We will never have to listen to anything again about "not winning it all." It will never be brought up again. But he never needed to win that game for me. Among coaches, consistency is even more important, and five Final Fours in 17 years is amazing. I'm extremely happy for him.

It's funny, but until this year I had never won the last game of the season. This will be special to me for the rest of my life. We would always come back to Kansas after going to the Final Four and people were excited and nice, but there's no comparison to winning it all. I've enjoyed every minute of it.

C. B. McGrath

This was my first season as an assistant coach with Coach Williams, after playing for him for four years at Kansas and working on his staff for a number of years.

I also coached the Carolina jayvees, which provided me with great experience in running a team.

For a college coach, the hardest thing to do is win consistently, as opposed to winning six games in a row. It takes a lot of luck, hard work, great players, and great coaching to win a national championship. But to run a program the way Coach Williams has run it for 17 years now, and to win with this percentage, is unbelievable. He never had to win a national championship to validate that he is a great coach. I would defend him to the day I die even if he did not win it, but beating Illinois makes it a little easier now.

Coach Williams treats everybody fairly, but not necessarily the same. You could have made 25 turnovers in practice and he could yell at you on every one of them, but once you leave the court he might say, "Good luck on your test" or "You'll have a better day tomorrow." There's no carryover. It's not just strictly basketball with him; he wants to know how you are doing in all facets of your life, and he tries to help you out, too. That's why he's so special.

McGrath (with the junior varsity team, opposite) played for Coach Williams at Kansas 1994–98.

149

Thirty-three wins and four losses and national champions—it doesn't get much better than that.

We started slow with the loss to Santa Clara, but we went to Maui and had a couple of good days of practice, and we got back on our horse. The players wanted to get better, had great attitudes, and went right to work.

Sometimes it's hard to get kids to understand how we want to push the ball, but once they figure it out, it's easy to play because you are so used to it. And it's definitely hard to play against us if we are playing that way. If we can get teams to shoot quickly, we can get up and down the court—and since we are used to doing that, it is easier for us to sustain it than it is for teams to block it off.

This group figured that out in Maui. Last year we would play that way at times, but then we would slow it down. In Maui we understood that we could do it [push the ball and run the court], and we did for three straight days. Maui scared a lot of teams that would play us later.

A big difference this year as opposed to last was that we had the confidence to win the close games. The Indiana game was huge for us. It was a real struggle where we were just grinding it out. It was on the road, a tough atmosphere, with everyone wanting us to lose Sean's hometown game. He didn't necessarily play great, but we found a way and toughed it out. That was huge—knowing that wherever we play, if we just do what Coach asks us to do, we have a chance to win.

Coach was able to use that Indiana win for the rest of the year. He always puts little reminders in guy's heads. He tries to use things that are fresh in their memory. He said, "We already won at Indiana, so we can win on the road."

Everybody that played for us was mentally tough.

Things would not go our way sometimes, but the players would bounce back.

They were focused on winning every game they could. We showed that toughness in beating Villanova in the Sweet 16. They were up big in the first half, and we needed something to change to go in our favor—a little 5-point run, where maybe Villanova would call a timeout and we could say, "Keep doing that for the next three minutes."

In games like that one, there is always a thought in the back of your mind: "Here we go again." I never made it to the Final Four as a player. At Kansas, we were a No. 1 seed three times and a No. 2 seed once. We always got upset by a team like Villanova that was on fire and never cooled off. This time Carolina did get some big stops, and we started scoring ourselves.

Coach really focused our kids on the defensive end in the week before the Final Four. We went into the practice gym and took the rims off. It was all defense. It wasn't throwing elbows; no one was trying to hurt somebody. It was getting your mind set to play defense on every possession if we want to win the national championship. We had to defend Michigan State if we wanted to win our next game, and the guys really bought in.

We needed to compete against Michigan State. I felt lucky to be down just 5 points at the half. We missed a few shots, weren't getting back on defense and weren't focused on guarding them. I don't know if it was first-half jitters for us in the Final Four, but Michigan State came out the aggressor. Coach told our players that if we *compete,* we have a chance. And our guys came out in the second half and competed like they did all year, and it worked out.

Both teams made runs in the championship game, but we made enough defensive stops at the end to win. Sean May played great in the final, capping one of the best months and a half I have ever seen. If you slice off the ACC Tournament, he was just phenomenal over the last 15 or so games. He put on a clinic against Illinois.

Our guys were determined to win the championship, and because of the hard work they put in to improving as a team, they deserved to win it.

JIM HAWKINS

JEFFREY A. CAMARATI

Steve Robinson

From day one, we talked about a "must-stop" on the defensive end of the floor.

We would do different drills, and all of a sudden Coach Williams would say, "Okay, you've got to get one stop—this is a must-stop drill." We knew at some point it would come down to that. It happened in the Duke game: We had to have a stop, and all of a sudden we got those stops we needed to give us a chance to win the game.

This Carolina team was hard for opponents to handle because it scored in bunches and attacked on both ends of the floor. It took a while for our players to understand what we wanted on defense. Our whole system—attacking on the offensive end of the floor, getting up and down the floor—was a big change for these guys. It's one thing to run when you have the ball. It's not quite as easy to run back, get in a stance, chase a guy around four screens, get hit and still keep chasing him, box out, rebound, then run the floor again. You could see early in the season that there was more of a commitment to playing that way. We might run one of our double-teams and get a steal, and then all of a sudden we would go on a 15-0 run.

We still hadn't learned that sometimes you have to grind it out for a full 40-minute type of game because we were able to put the hammer down on some people early. We were trying to teach our guys that consistently, every possession, you've got to be able to play. It all came to a head in the national

Robinson has spent 10 years on the bench with Coach Williams and was a Division I head coach for 7 years.

championship game, and our guys really did a nice job; at some crucial times when we had to have a stop, we got some stops.

We put a lot of pressure on opponents when they have the ball because if you take bad shots against us, all of a sudden there's a Sean May rebound, there's an outlet to Raymond Felton, there's a pitch ahead to one of our wings, and there's a dunk. Then you come back. We may trap you and steal the ball, then pitch it to somebody. There's a three. And all of a sudden, that's 5, that's 7, that's a 10-point run on you in less than 30 seconds, all because of one bad shot or being just a little careless with the basketball.

Two big differences from last year were our ability to win on the road and the way we handled adversity. It was maturity. Last year, if we had the lead and somebody came charging back at us, sometimes we didn't play with that poise and toughness to weather the storm and move forward. This year we knew that we could put points on the board and buckle down on defense and get a stop.

We had a sense of urgency to win the ACC regular-season championship.

You win one game, then you win another one . . . it became contagious. Our guys focused in, and it was important to Coach Williams. He's pretty competitive—driven about guys playing the best they can play—and getting the team prepared to play is one of the things that separate him from other coaches. I like to use the word *persistent.* He's persistent in all areas of the game. He wants our team to be persistent about how we attack and persistent about how we defend the screen, and not give in to "Well, I'm tired" or "I can't do it."

He's competitive, but I think his honesty, his sincerity, his caring for you as a person is why players feel the way they do about him. I don't think anybody could ever say he doesn't give it his all. As a player, you want to know that you're playing for a guy that's going to give you everything he's got everyday, trying to help make you a better team and a better player.

That was evident in Raymond's play. Last year I told him, "It'll be tough on you because you're used to

J. D. LYON JR.

154

free-wheeling, spinning, and Coach is trying to force-feed you into a little bit more of a thinking man's point guard role. Your second year will be so much easier because you're going to be more instinctive." And it *was* easier. The transition was like night and day. Raymond knocked down shots, shot a higher percentage, and did a better job taking care of the basketball. And as the season went on, he even got better. He started valuing the possession of the ball even more. His confidence grew, and the plays he made became more instinctive.

The way Jawad Williams played in the NCAA Tournament showed again the trust that developed between Coach Williams and the players. Jawad was hurt in the early rounds and didn't play at the level he had for much of the year, but then he had 20 points against Michigan State in the Final Four. There were many times at the end of the games during that stretch that Marvin was on the floor and Jawad wasn't. Jawad never complained about one thing. He was our biggest cheerleader because he wanted to win. He understood that this was his last opportunity, and he wasn't going to be selfish. He was all about what was best for our team at that time. Then he got his chance in the Final Four, and he delivered. That was his time to shine, and he certainly did.

Sean May played great throughout the NCAA Tournament and in the Final Four. About midseason he became more effective, and as he did, Sean's confidence grew and our team's confidence in Sean grew. They made more of an effort to get him the basketball, and he delivered.

We played an attacking man-to-man defense all year. Then we got to the national championship game and our zone defense was so important. We certainly didn't go into the game thinking we would play a lot of zone. But Raymond got his third foul, and all of a sudden we had to play zone to protect him. It led Illinois to shoot a high number of three-point shots. They wound up taking 40 three-point shots out of 72 shots total. That's a lot.

It all came down to that last timeout with a few minutes to play. Coach Williams told our players, "These are must-stops." That's what it boiled down to, and our guys got those key stops on the final possessions, and we won. Sometimes it's kind of hard to believe—you want to pinch yourself and say, "Man, we've won the national championship." It's just an unbelievable feeling.

JIM HAWKINS

Raymond Felton

Adapted from videotaped interviews

When I came to Carolina, I never had any individual goals—mainly just try to get a national championship.

This year was by far my best running the team, being the floor general. It clicked since the first game in Maui. It felt like we were together. Everyone was sharing the ball and doing all the little things.

Not playing against Santa Clara was tough. It's like being injured—you can't go out there and help your team. It was a situation where I made a mistake: I played in an unsanctioned basketball league. I learned from it, and I had to deal with the consequences.

When we got to Hawaii, Coach said, "We're not down here in Hawaii to have fun; we're down here for business, to win games and try to win the tournament. We're down here to handle business." I was definitely nervous when I hurt my wrist in Maui. I almost wanted to cry because the doctors didn't know for sure how serious it was. It seemed like it was a sprain, but

JEFFREY A. CAMARATI

Felton won the 2005 Bob Cousy Award as the nation's best point guard.

157

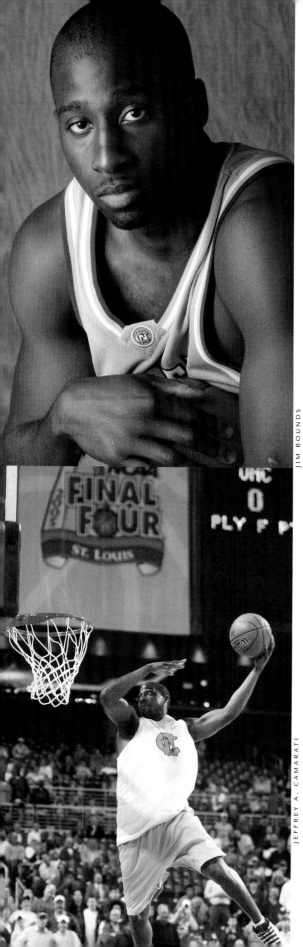

JIM BOUNDS

JEFFREY A. CAMARATI

they were going to check on it when we got home. It turned out to be just a little torn ligament, so I was like, "Forget it. Just keep wrapping it up. It's going to hurt regardless of whether I play tentative or I play hard—so forget it. I'll play the way I know how to play. And that's play hard."

Rashad and I came to an agreement this year.

We knew we were two of the biggest leaders. We knew we had to come together to make guys better and make them play. We said, "We've got to put everything behind us, in the past. We have to believe in Coach, listen to what he says and do what he says."

Early in the year we were just blowing teams out, and it didn't even seem like we were playing our best basketball. It's a lot of fun when you've got guys that can jump out of the gym, guys that shoot threes, big guys that can dominate inside. Any pass is not a bad pass because you've got guys who can hit shots, so it makes my job easy. It also makes it hard because you've got so many guys that can do things, and you are trying to keep them happy.

Playing point guard when the pace is this fast is a lot of pressure, but if you are trying to make plays, you are going to have some turnovers. You're running, you're passing, you're gunning . . . there are going to be some risky plays at times, but you have to make sure there are more good plays than bad plays.

This year I learned the game. My basketball IQ was definitely better, knowing how Coach Williams wants me to do things. I think I got the whole picture of the system and how he wants me to run the team. It took all of last year to learn that, but at the beginning of this season, I had a good understanding of what he wanted. We talked several times over the summer about things he wanted me to work on, things he wanted me to think about.

Coach Williams helped me learn the game from every aspect. He taught me not to worry about scoring, to play

PEYTON WILLIAMS

better defense, to play together as a team, just lead my team. He taught me how to be a guy that makes everybody on the court better, and get mine in between all of that.

I improved my shooting this year through hard work and not thinking about whether this was a good shot or a bad shot. I just took my time and shot the ball. Coach Williams gave me the green light—if I felt I was going to hit it, take it.

At Duke I could have at least gotten a shot off.

I was trying to let a play develop, but part of the play was for me to drive to the basket and make something happen.

Daniel Ewing made a risky try for a steal and he missed it, and I had the opportunity to drive to the basket and shoot a jumper or even go all the way. But I didn't take it. I backed out and looked for Rashad, and he was covered and Sean was covered, so I made a risky pass to David Noel and he just took off with it.

Looking back, it might have been a good thing because after that I had a chip on my shoulder, with an attitude that I was going to attack every team. I was going to play better, make things happen, and make sure we were going to win. That Duke loss did something to me.

A few weeks later at Maryland, we had a similar situation. I came off a ball screen; the lane was open, and I just took it all the way to the basket. Sean did a great job of sealing his man away so he couldn't get to my shot, and I had an open lay-up. I just attacked.

BOB DONNAN

JEFFREY A. CAMARATI

The fact I could be playing my last home game was definitely in my head from the beginning of the second Duke game, but toward the end it was all about just trying to win, trying to seal that ACC regular-season championship.

Down by 9, we believed we would win; we knew that game was not over no matter what. There was a three-minute stretch where Duke didn't score. Coach said to play defense every possession and get a good shot. It was my job to do that by penetration or by making their big guys come to me.

We lost focus in the ACC Tournament. We didn't play with intensity, with a fire, the desire—something you should never lose when you play a game. We lost that, and that's why we got put out so quickly in the second round. I knew we weren't playing our best basketball. But I think everything happens for a reason, and we came out in the NCAA Tournament playing with a chip on our shoulder—everybody. Everybody was going to do what we had to do to get this job done.

I knew I had to play well for us to go all the way, for us to win a national championship. I knew for a fact I had to do the best job for the next six games. But without Sean I don't think we would have won. He put on an amazing show in the last 15 games of the season, but in the NCAA Tournament he was the dominant player. Sean makes my job easier. It doesn't matter how you throw it in there—bounce pass, quick pass, high pass. Once he gets his hand on it, you know it's his, and you know he's going to finish.

In the second round we were glad to hear Iowa State say they wanted to run with us. I feel no team in the country can run with us—not the entire game. There's no team that is in better shape than we are. You may think we're tired, but we really are not. We're getting ready to turn it into another gear. We did that to Michigan State in the Final Four. They did a great job running with us in the first half and probably got the best of us in the first half. Then we just turned it up to a higher gear, and they couldn't run anymore. And that's how we took over the game.

> ## "No team in the country can run with us—not the entire game."

Before Illinois I thought, "This is what it's all about. It's what you dream of—what your childhood dreams are about.

You have a chance to seal the deal." I knew we had a big advantage inside with Sean. I was going to let my game come to me, get shots whenever I could. I was still going to attack like I did the whole season, but I was going to try and get the ball inside and let Sean do his work.

Tied at 65 [with 5:34 left to play], the shot clock was going down. Nobody was really open. Illinois was denying Sean aggressively inside, and I didn't want to make a risky pass. David Noel came over and set a screen; Deron Williams was late coming up on the screen, and he and Dee Brown jumped with me when I took the shot. But I had a good look at the basket, and it felt good from the time it left my hand. I knew it was going in. I have a

strong wrist; I've got great range. So I pulled up for the shot and had confidence I was going to hit it.

Illinois didn't drive to the basket to finish all year; they tend to drive to kick out for an open three-point shot. With 32 seconds left in the game, Luther Head had a wide open lay-up, but I believed in the scouting report. I knew Deron would be open for a three if I had come all the way in. So I kind of faked at Luther, and I knew he was going to try to throw it outside for an open three. I just kind of got my hand out there and got a steal.

Winning the championship was a dream come true. It's an unbelievable feeling I can't express with words.

Jackie Manuel

Coach Williams coming was a chance for me to start over, a new opportunity to show people that whatever negative things you heard about me, that's not the case.

A chance to show you that I'm willing to buy into anything. I'm not the type of guy that fights against the system. That's why it was easier for me to buy into the system than maybe some other people.

Coach Williams is a great coach. He's going to teach you the fundamentals of the game, and off the court he cares about his kids. He wants the best for his kids. He's going to push you; he's trying to bring the best out of you. When he got to Carolina, he told me, "This is nothing personal, but looking at the numbers, they're not good. We're going to limit your shooting but work on the things that you're strong at. You keep working on your shot; we're going to have the coaches help you and get it better." I understood that my numbers weren't that great. So I took that constructive criticism and went on.

KEVIN COX/WIRE IMAGE

Manuel started 85 of 126 games and averaged 6.2 points per game as a Tar Heel.

167

JEFFREY A. CAMARATI

Playing great defense did give me a chance to make an impact.

At the beginning of my career, I got labeled as a guy who's not a great shooter. That label stuck with me, and it's hard to fight. However, the defensive label really helped me. Instead of people saying, "He can't shoot," they praised me for my defense.

Defense is all about desire, determination, heart. You have the determination to stop a guy and the mentality that nobody's going to score on you. It's not any special technique. It's something I never worked on in my life; it's just something I was blessed with. Even in high school, I hated for people to score on me and that carried over once I got to UNC.

I watch tape. I read the coaches' report. I do my own scouting report and try to find my opponent's strengths and weaknesses. I break down everything he likes to do—which way he likes to dribble; if he likes to go one dribble to the left and pull up; if he can't go right and pull up. It's all about pride. The night before a game, I think about how many points he averages. If he's averaging 15 or 20 points, I'm trying to hold him under 10 because to me, holding a guy under his average is just like scoring.

Two guys I enjoyed competing against had to be Julius Hodge and J. J. Redick. Every time I went against those guys, I tried to have my best game, make sure I was ready mentally and physically. Especially with Julius, because if he gets any kind of edge on you, he's going to let you know about it, and that's one thing I didn't want him to do. I tried to be ready.

In the last Duke game, the first half was crazy. I wondered, "Is J. J going to miss?" I'm making the shots as tough as possible, but he's shooting fade-aways, and I'm thinking, "Well, if he's playing like this in the second half, this game might get ugly because I'm doing everything I can to stop him." I didn't realize until after the game he didn't even score in the second half.

Most guys who get defensive awards are guys who block shots, guys who make steals. But they don't have to be great defenders to do that. You can gamble on defense if you're quick enough and you can get steals, but it still doesn't mean you're a great defender. To run around and chase guys around screens, guard the top players—knowing they have the green light and can shoot anytime they want—that's tough.

That's why my favorite defensive play is denying the guy the ball. If you deny the guy the ball, especially the top scorer, he gets frustrated. That's what I try to do every time.

> **To me, holding a guy under his average is just like scoring.**

That last home game felt good—getting the chance to beat Duke, be regular-season champions, and cut the nets down.

I was very excited about that. But in the back of my mind, I knew we still had some business to finish, so I didn't go overboard with my celebration.

Coming back to practice, we were rusty and I was thinking, "This is not looking good at all, but maybe once we get to D.C. everybody will step up and we'll be okay." We figured we would probably face Maryland in the ACC Tournament. We were not thinking about playing Clemson, and once we did I think everybody relaxed. But it was a different Clemson team, and we just had a dogfight.

After we lost in the ACC Tournament, Coach Williams took us back to the beginning, to the practices we had after the loss to Santa Clara. We refocused and said, "We lost. We can't worry about it now; it's time to move on." The NCAA Tournament is not something you can go into and say, "Oh, if we lose, we've got another tournament." No, if we lose, we're out. Everybody understood that, and that's why we were so sharp, that's why we were so determined. Coach Williams gets a lot of that credit because he worked our butts off.

We had that fire in Charlotte [for the first and second rounds of the NCAA Tournament] that we had in the beginning of the season. Everybody was bringing their A game on both ends. I knew it was going be tough for any team, especially with just one or two scorers, to beat us. I knew we were back on track, especially when Marvin and Raymond saved the ball and I got a lay-up against Oakland. Guys were hustling, putting their bodies out there. To have the fans behind us felt like we were at the Smith Center again. After that, guys said, "We can do this; let's go on ahead and win the whole thing."

We were glad to hear Iowa State talk about running with us. Everybody's saying, "Okay, Carolina runs, but we

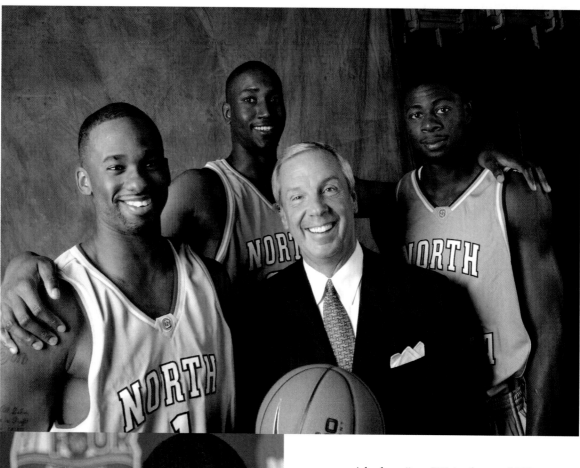

can run with them" or "We're better." What those teams didn't understand is that we were not just running on offense, but on both ends of the court. Most teams, once they have the ball in their hands, then yes—everybody's going to run because everybody wants the ball; everybody wants to score. But who's going to get back?

We established that early: "Okay you want to run, let's run. But we're going to run both ends." And they weren't really expecting that. So now we're forcing Iowa State to do something they're not used to doing. Now they have to spend all their energy trying to get back on defense and they have none on offense. With the rotation where we were subbing guys in and out, it just killed them—they just ran out of steam.

Villanova came out with a chip on their shoulder.

I don't know if we were still celebrating from the wins in Charlotte, but we had to get rid of that real quick because those guys were on fire.

It didn't matter if you had a hand in their faces or if you were tugging on them—they were knocking down some big shots. It was a dogfight, another game where we had to play to the end.

I was telling myself, "If we win this game, if we pull this one out, then it's meant to be. We're going to win it all." Because they had our number; they really did.

We knew at halftime against Wisconsin that if we didn't come out and play hard, play smart, then we were going home. Big May stood up and shouted, "Twenty minutes. The first half is over; all we got is 20 minutes," and I think everybody started to understand that. Everybody shook their heads and came out like, "Let's go. We came too far to say we're just going to tuck it in."

The Final Four was nerve-wracking. Everybody is at home watching; everybody is in the Dome watching—all eyes are on you. Everybody's going to see every little mistake you make. It was that nervous energy; the guys were saying, "Oh my goodness, I can't breathe. I don't know how these guys from Michigan State are doing it, but they're killing us. They're kicking our butts up and down the court."

It was a tough first half because what we usually do to other teams, Michigan State was doing to us: They were running us up and down the court. Jawad was keeping us in the game, but guys were out there sucking wind. We were down in the first half by 5, and we went into the locker room saying to ourselves, "We have come this far; we're here in the Final Four. We've got to go out there and play."

The second half was our half—what they were doing to us in the first half, we started doing to them. And the difference was that Michigan State got fatigued. Some teams will only run one half and they can't run the whole game. We just started out-running them, subbing guys in and out, and they were in trouble.

My job in the championship game was to limit three-point shots because that's Illinois' game: They penetrate, kick the ball out, and knock down the three-pointers.

The goal is to limit their three-point shots, get the ball into Sean, and get their big guys in foul trouble. Well, they don't miss to start the second half. These guys are picking me off and I'm asking the officials, "Is that a moving screen?" Because I'll pick my path and avoid the first guy, and then the second guy just picks me off, and he gets wide-open shots.

I was telling myself, "We still have the lead; relax and keep playing. Don't worry about the officials; don't worry about anything." When Illinois started cutting on our lead and everybody was getting a little nervous, I wanted to pull my hair out because I was either getting a foul call or getting nailed.

Once time ran out, it was a shock to me. I needed somebody to pinch me because it really seemed like it wasn't happening. I kept saying, "This can't be." Jawad, Melvin, and I have been through a lot. We hugged up, and Jawad started praying and crying. Coach Williams came over. He's always been criticized for not winning the "big game." It just felt like we were all in the same boat and we all accomplished our goals and did what people said we couldn't do.

Looking back on my four years at Carolina, it's been great. If I had another opportunity, I would do it all over again in a heartbeat. I'm really going to miss it. I've had so much fun interacting with different people, meeting new people, and it's tough to say goodbye to this place. You hear guys talk about it all the time and it really doesn't sink in until it's your time to go—how much you're going to miss this place, and the memories you have.

Manuel and his fiancée, Ronda Norman, at Commencement. They were married on August 13, 2005.

Sean May

Adapted from videotaped interviews

JEFFREY A. CAMARATI

Coach Williams changed people's perception about me. People didn't realize that under all this huge, burly body fat, there is an athlete.

I made some athletic plays this year because I was in better shape. He got me to key in on my favorite counter-moves, get my post moves solid. He told me once that I was a jack of all trades, master of none. Now people can say about me, "He's got a nice jump hook, got a great turnaround jump shot, can pass the ball, can do a lot of good things." Coach allowed me to be successful—he put me in positions to be successful. He pulled out my strengths and hid my weaknesses. And Coach taught me how to run the floor. I never wanted to know until I came here, but now I love it.

Through the NCAA Tournament, it happened that I was playing well. Sometimes you get on a streak. I was very confident going into the NCAA Tournament, and I kept it going the whole way. I was in better shape also, and I was

May averaged 17.5 points and 10.7 rebounds per game in his final season. He was named Final Four MVP.

177

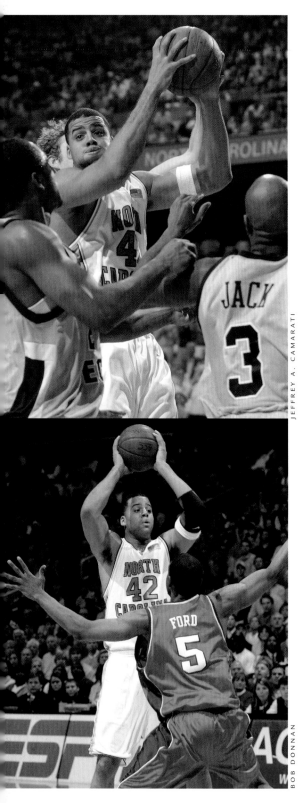

lighter. I wasn't tired at the end of this season like I was last year. Those plays I made in the Elite Eight and the Final Four were because I was a lot fresher than I was last year.

I felt nobody could guard me. If I got the ball, we had a great chance of scoring. My teammates had confidence in me, and Coach had confidence in me. Anytime you are getting praise from your coaches and your teammates and you are shooting a high percentage and you're being successful, it just keeps adding on. You have guys running over to tell Coach, "Give him the ball and he'll get it done."

Playing with a great point guard like Raymond is about as easy as it can get. If Ray's going to the lane and drops the ball off to me, I've got a wide-open lay-up. There was a play in the first half of the Illinois game where he dribbled right over half court and we locked eyes for a good five seconds. He dribbled to the left and knew exactly when to throw it. When you have that chemistry, it's hard to beat. For teams to win championships, you've got to have a dominant inside player and a great point guard. You can get other pieces of the puzzle to fit in, but if you don't have those two, it's hard to win games.

Plus, we have great shooters. That makes it extremely hard to double-team us, and that's what Illinois found out.

Before the season started I sat down with my dad and we talked about the key games where you've really got to play well.

You want to play well all the time, but you want to stand out in the Duke games. I know the history of the rivalry and people at Carolina; beating Duke is like a national championship to them. We didn't win that first game against them, but I felt I played pretty well. Before the second game, I said to myself, "Play like it's your last because you never know." To go out with 26 points and 24 rebounds in my last game in the Dean Dome was a great way to end my career.

178

The crazy thing about beating Duke is we walked over to the huddle for the last TV timeout, and you could look into everybody's eyes—last year, you could see it in people's eyes when we thought we were going to lose games—and you would have thought we were up by 10. Everybody was cool, calm, and collected. Coach said, "I promise you, if you play defense the way you know how to play, we'll be there in the end." That's exactly what happened. It was the most bizarre game I've ever been a part of. But it's the best game I've ever been a part of—except for the national championship game.

We knew our whole goal was to win a national championship.

After we lost to Georgia Tech in the ACC Tournament, we were in the locker room and either Jackie or Jawad said, "We didn't come here to win the ACC Tournament title. We came here to win a national championship. Everybody get your mind right. Let's get back to playing the way we were playing before. And let's go at this thing next week." That's exactly what we did.

We scared people with those two NCAA Tournament games in Charlotte—the way we were running. And we had a guy [Marvin Williams] coming off the bench, getting 20 points both games. That scared a lot of teams.

Villanova has us by double figures late in the first half. The crazy thing about our team is that you would never see doubt at any time. We were down 13, guys were still making mistakes, and we weren't playing well. We go in at halftime and Coach says, "Just find a way. If you want to win a national championship, find a way." We chipped away at it piece by piece.

Going into Wisconsin, I was a little nervous because Mike Wilkinson is a great talent. He's got footwork—I saw him do things that not a lot of players can do. Everybody said, "You've got your work cut out for you tomorrow." I took that as a slap in the face; I didn't think my teammates had confidence in me. Right before the tip, Rashad comes up and says, "Man, he's too little for you. If you don't kill him, we don't win this game." I took that as motivation.

BOB DONNAN

> **The crazy thing about our team is that you would never see doubt at any time.**

J. D. LYON JR.

179

We were tied at the half, but Coach Holladay told me coming out of halftime, "We're going to have to ride your back if we are going to win this game." I came out and scored the next 8 points and got 4 or 5 rebounds. Later, in the huddle, Melvin said, "Coach, don't draw up anything. Get the ball to Sean—that's all we've got to do."

I was kind of frustrated when Coach took the rims off in practice before the Final Four. You're at the latter part of the season, and you're getting ready to go to the Final Four—you don't really want to be in there doing defensive drills that you haven't done since the beginning of the season. But Coach was trying to instill that defensive mentality again because that's what was going to make us successful. I think it really helped us. I think we keyed in and played a lot better defense against Michigan State and Illinois.

I spoke to my dad the night before the championship game.

He said, "There is one game left. You know what to do; go get it done. You have a chance to do something special." He gets more nervous than I do, so he didn't want to talk too much.

My mom threw a surprise 21st-birthday party for me in the elevator lobby on our floor at the team hotel. It helped calm everybody down. It took our minds off the game—allowed us to be around friends and family, laugh a little bit, have fun. And then we all went back to our rooms and got ready for the game. I definitely think it helped take some of the tension away.

Normally I wake up at 7:00, 8:00 in the morning. The day of the Illinois game, I woke up about 4:00 A.M. I just sat there and stared at the ceiling and thought about the game. I ran the game through my mind about a hundred times— everything I was going to do, who I was playing against. I've never had an experience like that. The funny thing is, I didn't sleep but I wasn't tired, and it all worked out in the end.

I thought Illinois would start Roger Powell on me. If they ran Powell at me, I could see over the top of him and hit guys coming out of the double-team. If they ran a bigger guy at me, it made it a little more difficult. I got really deep in the paint; Ray threw the ball over a couple of times, and I was scoring before the double-team could actually come. We were so in tune with throwing the ball into the post. Whether it was Marvin, Jawad, or me, we were going to get the ball inside. That was the difference in the game.

Winning Final Four MVP means a lot to me because it shows the hard work I put in. I don't think any player in the country breaks down tape more than I do. After every game, I get the tape from Coach, and before we even watch it as a team, not only do I watch my mistakes, I watch other people. I look at plays from Raymond's point of view or from Rashad's—to see what they see—so that I can understand them, so that I can develop a better relationship on the floor with them. When you do those types of things and you're successful, it means a lot.

Coach [Phil] Ford was the main reason I came to Carolina. I knew there was somebody I could trust and who would look out for me. He called me after we won and he said, "Man, do you realize people are going to forget about me now? You guys did something special that a lot of players couldn't

ROBERT CRAWFORD

ARMIN DASTUR

RONALD MARTINEZ / GETTY

do. They're going to stop talking about Phil Ford. They're going to be talking about Raymond Felton and Sean May, Rashad McCants . . ." I just told him, "Hey man, don't be jealous. I'll still remember you."

Coming to Carolina is the best decision I've ever made.

People in this community opened their arms to me. I was lost coming from Indiana, didn't know what to expect. There was a point my freshman year when I thought about leaving Carolina because I wasn't sure where things were going to go with my career after I'd gotten hurt. A lot of people close to this program told me to stick around, that this university needed me to be here. It's a place I can always say I love. It's a place I can always call home, where I can see myself living for a long time. I'm forever grateful for my memories here and the people I've met here, the relationships I've developed. It's something I'll cherish for the rest of my life.

Whenever I come back, people are going to know me because I was on a *national championship* team. I was talking to somebody yesterday, and there was this six- or seven-year-old with him. When that kid is 20 years old, going to school here, I'll come back and he'll come up to me and say, "I used to watch you when I was little and I used to love you and the way you played." That's part of the greatest memory—that you'll have an impact on people you never met and who aren't your age, kids who are four, five, six, seven years old and just starting to learn the game. And one of the reasons they'll want to come to Carolina is they saw you play.

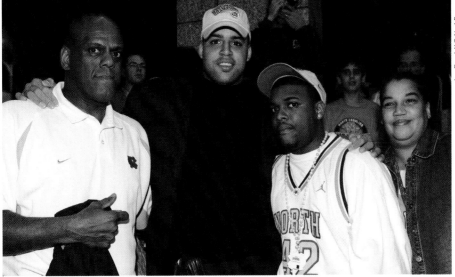

The May family after the national championship game.

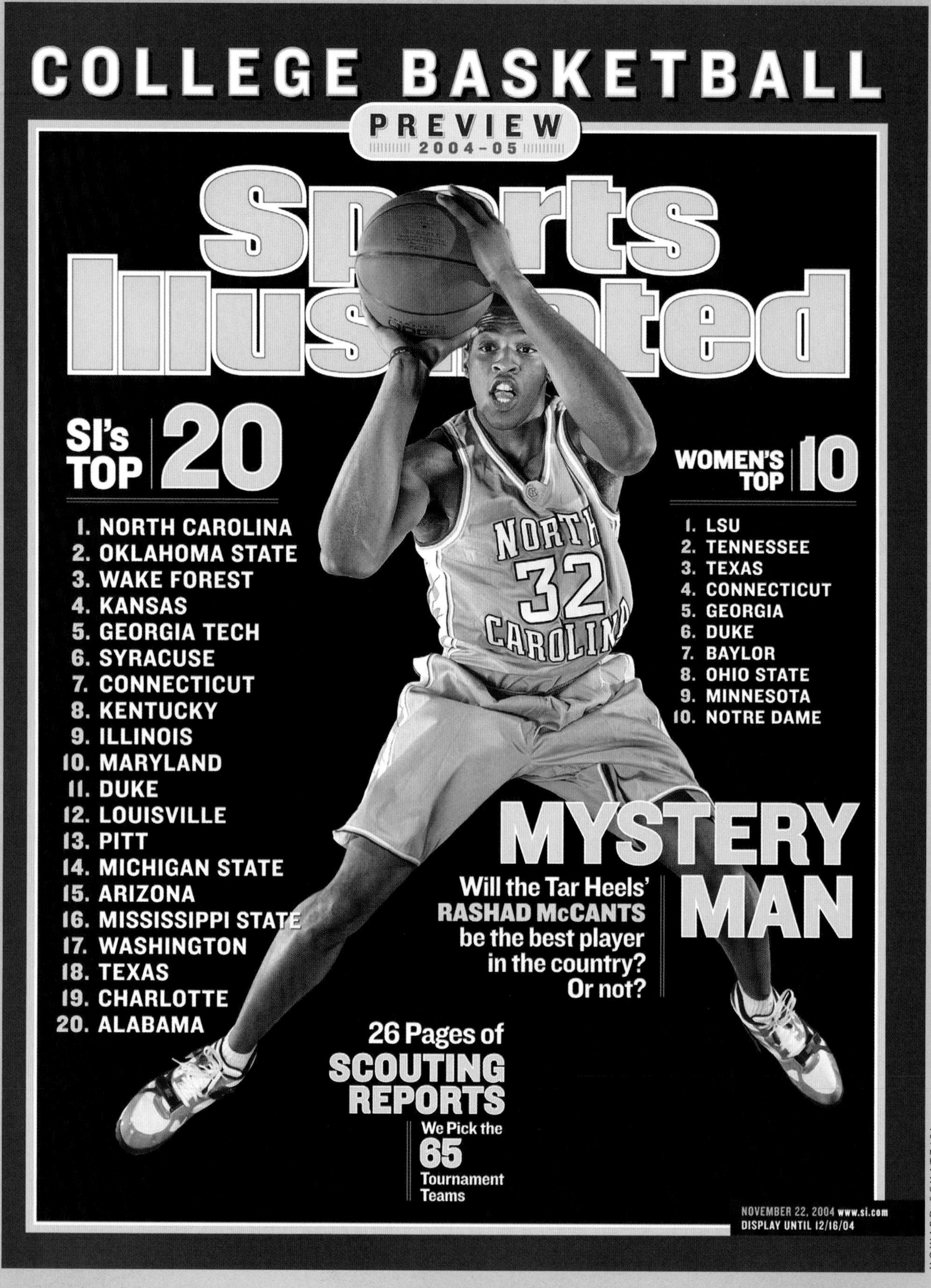

COLLEGE BASKETBALL

PREVIEW
2004–05

Sports Illustrated

SI's TOP 20

1. NORTH CAROLINA
2. OKLAHOMA STATE
3. WAKE FOREST
4. KANSAS
5. GEORGIA TECH
6. SYRACUSE
7. CONNECTICUT
8. KENTUCKY
9. ILLINOIS
10. MARYLAND
11. DUKE
12. LOUISVILLE
13. PITT
14. MICHIGAN STATE
15. ARIZONA
16. MISSISSIPPI STATE
17. WASHINGTON
18. TEXAS
19. CHARLOTTE
20. ALABAMA

WOMEN'S TOP 10

1. LSU
2. TENNESSEE
3. TEXAS
4. CONNECTICUT
5. GEORGIA
6. DUKE
7. BAYLOR
8. OHIO STATE
9. MINNESOTA
10. NOTRE DAME

MYSTERY MAN

Will the Tar Heels'
RASHAD McCANTS
be the best player
in the country?
Or not?

26 Pages of
SCOUTING REPORTS

We Pick the
65
Tournament
Teams

NOVEMBER 22, 2004 www.si.com
DISPLAY UNTIL 12/16/04

HOWARD SCHATZ/SI

Rashad McCants

Adapted from videotaped interviews

JIM HAWKINS

Last year when we lost to Texas, we got in a room and said if we want to win, we all have to put this jealous stuff behind us and just play as a team.

Everyone had an agreement that whatever it took, you were going to do. *Whatever it took.* If you were going to sacrifice getting awards, you do it. If you had to sacrifice getting rebounds, you do it. If you had to sacrifice getting points, you do it.

I knew what I had to do to help my team win a championship. But at the same time I was hoping the world knew my sacrifices were for the good of

McCants averaged 16 points per game in his final season.

the team. Instead of coming back and averaging 25 points, average 15—that's all I was really thinking about.

I always felt I was a good defensive player. Stepping up and making big plays this year is all I wanted to do, whether it be a block, steal, rebound, anything—as long as I can get in there and make something happen for my team. I think that's what makes me so dangerous.

On offense, I'm thinking, "Get me the ball and set me a screen," because as long as I get the ball, I have a chance to score. That's what goes through my head. When you have the ball on the floor, you have to be the cockiest, most confident player in the world. If you are not, they will take it away from you. That's how I am. I feel no one can stop me when I have the ball. I feel that it has a 99.9 percent chance of going in. And the times I miss it is something I did wrong. There isn't anything somebody can do to alter my shot or make me miss. That's why I always want the ball when there are three seconds, two seconds, 0.6—whatever.

There's only one way to become a good shooter: just shoot. That's all I do. I got some advice from an old mentor back in Asheville. He told me if you shoot in a gym you call your home, then make sure you shoot from everywhere—so if you pull up in a game, you're not thinking, "Well I never shot here before." So you shoot everywhere, as many times as you can, and you play horse by yourself and you keep shooting and you keep shooting.

I wanted to make sure fans got their money's worth. I loved watching people sit down, coming to their seats, being there early for shootaround. That's the best part—the people. The people make the game fun. That's why we are playing, to entertain. And to get confidence, you have to get attention—and I love attention. Me being the first one out there on the court, with people giving me attention, gives me the confidence to keep shooting and keep wanting to make it. People give me more attention when I make more shots. That just makes me work harder. The crowd feeds and feeds and I become stronger and better—and that's why I love the crowd.

After the Santa Clara game, Raymond and I talked on the way out of San Francisco to Maui.

We talked and we fixed a lot of things. It was an agreement between two players with high basketball IQs. We didn't come here to lose; we came here to win championships, so we have to lead this team. So we just said, "We are going to get this done, and we aren't going to let anybody become an excuse for our failure." And we got it done, and it was just wonderful to see.

After what we did in Maui, nobody could touch us. I knew that for a fact. It wasn't that we beat teams—it was the *way* we beat two teams [Tennessee and Iowa] that could compete with anybody else in the country.

Practices in Maui were hot and humid, and everybody was just constantly sweating. It was slippery on the floor, and we did defensive stations 60 percent of the practice. Everybody was dog-tired. It was the hardest practice I've ever done for two days straight. I think that was probably one of the greatest coaching moves I've ever seen—for Coach Williams to push us the way he did and make us realize we weren't there for vacation, we were there for business. It

> **To get confidence, you have to get attention—and I love attention.**

JEFFREY A. CAMARATI

really juiced everybody up to let him know that we messed up once, but we probably weren't going to mess up too many more times.

Coach Williams pretty much fixed all the things I was having trouble with. He learned I would do anything he asked me to do on the court. Once he figured out there wasn't anything to my facial expressions, that's when everything picked up. We started winning, winning, winning.

I scored 28 in a big win over Kentucky, but I feel I've been heavily criticized for just being a scorer or offensive player, and I wanted to change those perceptions. I was coming on strong the first five or six games and I could have continued that, but I didn't want my teammates to feel unimportant on the floor. So I looked in the mirror and told myself that I was going to play better defense—better than anyone else on the team. And I was going to get guys involved to the point where they would always look for the ball when I had it.

I most definitely put too much pressure on myself at Duke.

I knew I had to have a good game. If I didn't have a good game, the whole world was just going to collapse . . . I was hyped about the game. I felt I needed to prove that I was the best player in the country. It was just a lot of pressure.

After we didn't get a shot off in the final seconds of the game, Raymond and I were sitting there saying, "We cannot keep losing to these guys by 1 point. We cannot keep doing this. It hurts too bad to come over to Cameron and lose by 1 point when you are supposed to win."

Not knowing I was sick [with an intestinal disorder] at the time, I felt I didn't show up for the game. I wasn't myself at all. I made a couple of shots, but I just didn't play the way I know I can play. That was the frustrating thing. After the game, I was like, "How did I let this guy drive me like that?" or "How did I not block his shot?" I was looking for an excuse to say I should have played better.

JEFFREY A. CAMARATI

JEFFREY A. CAMARATI

I was fatigued constantly. During the Duke game I was coming out every two minutes or so. I didn't know what was going on because I got winded a lot quicker than I usually do. I'm the type of player who plays five to six minutes at a time, but it was really bothering me. I couldn't shoot from as deep as I wanted and I was used to, and I didn't have my legs. I remember air-balling at Connecticut. That's when I really knew something was wrong.

It was tremendously hard to miss those four games at the end of the regular season. Knowing you are supposed to be on the floor, helping your team win, is very hard. On Senior Day I wanted to be out there on the floor with the guys. I knew that was going to be my last home game and I wasn't going to be able to play in it—and it was against Duke. I had been circling that on the calendar forever. For me not to be able to play—that hurt. It hurt from the beginning. But to see Melvin, Jawad, and Jackie go out like that was touching.

Winning the national championship means that all the preparation we have done to get to that point has paid off.

Sometimes during the year, at our practices, we did the same thing every day. You keep wondering to yourself, "If we continue to keep doing stuff like this every day, is it really going to pay off? Are we really going to win the championship?" And later you sit back and think, "All the things we did were perfect for us." You have to commend a coach for understanding that. Coach Williams just designed something perfect for a bunch of players who had never won anything, and for us to do everything that we've done in this short period of time is amazing.

The first feeling I had when we beat Illinois was satisfaction. Finally, we reached the goal that everyone has been working so hard for. It's breath-taking.

When you listen to the song "One Shining Moment," you think of being a player at Carolina. You remember everything you've done, especially on the basketball court, in the weight room—all the places you've been with the team, all the plays you've run, all the practices you've had, all the meetings, tape . . . you remember all of those things. There were some practices when you ran too much or did too many defensive stations, but when the day is over, if you are a basketball player and you love to play, then you can remember Carolina as something greater than life.

David Noel

Adapted from videotaped interviews

The biggest thing we had to correct from last year was our selfishness.

And we had to buy into the whole defensive belief Coach was trying to preach. I felt that if we could get everybody to play defense and help each other out like we did in practice, and convert that to a game, then nobody could beat us.

We finally got the commitment from everybody during the preseason workouts—because they were atrocious. It was that bad. We all pulled together and said, "All right, we know what we have to do, so let's get it done." Everybody had that same attitude throughout the rest of the conditioning program, and that's what definitely tipped it off.

Plenty of guys made sacrifices. Rashad made the first and the biggest step, because a lot of the things Rashad was doing last year, he stepped back from this year. He bought into the defensive aspect of the game. That helped us in being the cohesive defensive team that we could have been

BOB DONNAN

Noel blossomed into a defensive stopper as a junior, often teaming with Manuel to guard the opposing team's top player.

193

last year, but weren't. Sean sacrificed a lot of his eating habits to get his body better. That boy, he did what he had to do to help this team—and that's what everybody did this year.

Last year a lot of guys rested on defense. This year when we got the added depth with Quentin Thomas, Reyshawn Terry, and definitely Marvin, guys were like, "All right, let's give it all we got on both ends."

My role was the second defensive stopper because we knew Jackie was the first. When you've got a guy like Jackie guarding your best player and then you have me coming off the bench, it's definitely going to be tough for an opponent. Marvin rotating with Sean and Jawad allowed me to play the 3 [small forward], and that helped me a lot because it was hard banging down there with those big dudes. Guarding perimeter players is more my style.

It's nice to hear people say that I handled not playing as much as I would like with a lot of class.

That's something you just smile about. When you hear people speak like that about you, you think, "My mama did a great job raising me." That's definitely where that comes from.

I went and talked to Coach Williams about playing time. Before the Vermont game he said, "You're doing everything we need you to do. You're doing a great job," and I felt good about it. Then I played about eight minutes against Vermont. I talked to him the next day and he said, "Don't worry about it. You're doing everything right." I just needed to know that so I could keep my head focused.

The guys on our team tend to get down on themselves sometimes. They tend to think of all the negatives instead of the positives. One of the guys that stepped up as a speaking leader was Jackie. As soon as I said something, he backed me up. Everybody else got in that mode where everything turned from negative to positive. And we kept that same attitude all year.

The first Duke game crushed us. Being down the whole game, and then to actually have a chance to win it at the end and not even get a shot off—that hurt us a lot. Coach took that loss to Duke back to practice and changed our attitude about certain situations. We focused on the little things we needed to do because those little things are what kept us from winning those games.

Raymond was really down after the loss in Cameron. He got back in the gym and said, "Man, I need to go back to the basics." He went back to handling the ball like he normally handled the ball, and he worked on his jumper a lot more. Raymond turned it on and left it on for the rest of the season.

We said from the beginning of the year that we wanted to win the ACC outright because we hadn't won it in forever. Then Rashad got sick and missed the last four games of the regular season. Melvin came out and had some great games when Rashad got sick, so that took the pressure off everybody else. I was playing a whole lot more minutes, which helped me, especially my confidence. When we were winning without Rashad, we realized, "This is how much of a team we are. We can win without one of our best players. And when he comes back, nothing is going to change." That's the way we looked at it.

I had a good game defensively at NC State, scored 12 points at Maryland, and had 8 assists against FSU and a big steal against Duke. I told myself, "Dave, this is your chance. Go out here and have a good game. You don't have to go out here and match what Rashad does; just go out and play the way you know how to play." It's different when you don't feel pressure on yourself. I started to have fun, and that's the way I played for the rest of the season—just having fun and relaxing.

Jackie and I had the responsibility of guarding J. J. Redick in the rematch with Duke. We didn't pay attention to how many points he had until halftime, when Coach came in and said, "J. J. had 17." We said, "This dude ain't scoring another bucket." Once we got that mentality—with Jack on you first and then me coming off the bench—it's like, "You're going to get tired before we do." We wore Redick down a little bit and kind of discouraged him from taking shots.

We had a timeout when we were down by 2 points. We came out of the timeout, and we were supposed to switch every screen. But I messed up and didn't switch off on Danny Ewing, and that's how Duke even got the ball in bounds. All I was trying to do was cut them off, and I was about to foul. I actually let Ewing go past me and I just reached around, got a good piece of the ball, and was able to knock it loose. Raymond dove on it, and we were able to get the ball back. We called a timeout and all I could do was just say, "Thank you, God," because that was a big play for us. Coach had just told me to never again reach around for a steal—and I did it anyway.

Melvin and I were partially responsible for us getting to the Final Four.

Wisconsin had a big man [Mike Wilkinson] with a lot of moves, and Melvin and I were giving Sean the business. We said, "He's going to kill you. He's going to hit you with a jump hook fade-away." We were making up stupid stuff. Sean said, "Okay, I'm going to show you." Right before the game, I said to Sean, "Uh-oh, it's time. Don't be scared. He's coming for you." And Sean went out and had one of the best games of his life.

All we heard on Sunday [the day before the championship game] was whether or not we were a team. What more did we have to prove for us to be a team? For them to keep saying we didn't have chemistry, that we weren't together, was totally preposterous to me.

The Illinois game went backwards for us. Our first half was so great, but in the second half Illinois started making threes, which brought them back into the game. Usually it's the flip side—a team comes out and sticks with us in the first half, and then we blow them out in the second half. But it was a great game—a high-octane game where they were making runs, we were making runs—and it all came down to the biggest plays. We made them in the end to get the win.

> **Coach had just told me to never again reach around for a steal—and I did it anyway.**

Raymond made a big three and got a steal to help us win. Right before his steal, we were coming out of the huddle and I said, "I'm about to get a steal." I thought about it and said, "No, *we're* about to get a steal." I looked at Raymond, and sure enough, he got a steal. I wondered, "How in the world did that just happen?" It was like God had sent me a message. Ray took the ball down, knocked down some big free throws, and continued to make free throws. And we were jumping on the floor at the end.

It's incredible to celebrate on the floor with your team and watch *One Shining Moment* on the big screen. One of my favorite plays of the year was when Ray threw me a long bounce pass and I dunked on Michigan State. Ray threaded the needle, and it fell right into my hand—all I did was jump and dunk it. Man, I was happy. I was thinking, "I hope that gets me on *One Shining Moment*."

They showed the play, and I said, "Hey, that's me!" You really can't explain it. It's one of those things you don't even dream about. I thought, "Wow, I'm definitely blessed to be in this situation right now because God has truly put the ball in my court and said, 'Here—just run with it.' And He's carried me the whole way."

Playing at Carolina has meant everything.

The people here are so great around Franklin Street, on campus, off campus. You don't have any really bad days. When you do have bad days, there are people here to pick you up. Just being around this program, being around the people here, is something I'll cherish for the rest of my life.

Even when I go away I'll come back to Chapel Hill because a part of it is in me. When you have that type of close-knit relationship with a place, it's hard to leave. That played a big factor in Coach Williams coming back. He spent so much time here, and when he went to Kansas for 15 years, that piece of Carolina was still calling him—and that's why he had to come back. The tradition of Carolina basketball is big. For me to be a part of that, I can't even put it into words. Being in the same sentence as Michael Jordan, James Worthy, Coach Smith, Coach Williams, and Raymond Felton . . . that's something big.

RONALD MARTINEZ/GETTY

ELSA/GETTY

Melvin Scott

Adapted from videotaped interviews

JEFFREY A. CAMARATI

When the NCAA Tournament began, I saw this belt at the mall that you could program to display whatever you wanted.

I said, "I've got to have that." I programmed it and was ready to go. That's just what I needed for the Final Four. At the official salute banquet, guys were uptight. So when we went on stage to get our rings and watches, I had my belt on, flashing "Final Four." I showed off the belt, and everybody started laughing. I think that loosened the guys up.

I told the guys back at the hotel, "You act like y'all have been here before, but I've never been here, so I'm going to enjoy all of this." We were the more relaxed team at the Final Four. That was key to us winning the whole thing because we had great talent and we had fun, but at the same time, we took care of business. When you take care of business and have fun with it, that's when you do your best.

We knew what we had to do at the start of the year to get to that position. It was a matter of us being unselfish and sharing the ball. Even in pick-up games, the guys that shared the ball were the ones that won the games.

Scott is seventh in school history in career three-pointers; he made 45 in his senior season.

201

> "For us to win the championship, the only guys who went 8 and 20, says a lot about us."

We learned a lot from ourselves, with Coach Williams leading us.

Fighting through all the adversity and winning the national championship says a lot about our character and our heart—especially, Jackie, Jawad, and me. A lot of people criticized our class. They said, "You're the worst class ever, the class that brought the program down." I always wanted to come here. I've been struggling all my life, and losing basketball games wasn't going to make me run away from my problems. So for us to win the championship and still be standing, the only guys that went 8 and 20, says a lot about us. People can respect us for that.

Winning is great, but it is hard to not play as much as you want to or think you should.

I went from playing about 33 minutes to 13 minutes a game this year. That's tough for anyone, but it was for the good of the team. My freshman or sophomore year, I would have flipped out. But because I'm mature, I was able to handle it for the championship run. I realized, "Hey, I can only control what I can control myself. When my opportunity comes, I need to get out there and play; I need to do my best." We were winning games, we were doing fine, and I didn't want to be that bad apple in the bunch.

I didn't crack the lineup until Rashad got sick late in the season. I knew it was a lot of pressure and I had to prove myself. My teammates got me going in the right situations where I could shoot the ball, and I never lost my confidence. Just put me in the lineup and get me the ball—that was the easiest part.

Our team really matured this year as well. It was a matter of us going through tough times and being in tough situations, maybe getting frustrated at each other—but then coming together. We've been in a lot of tough situations. In previous years we weren't able to pull some games out, but building trust in each other this year was the key to our success.

Carolina going into the NCAA Tournament close to home and winning big shocked a lot of people because of how we played in the ACC Tournament. I think we faked people out. We were tired in the ACC Tournament. I know a lot of people thought we're going down at the NCAAs. To be close to home and start blasting guys and running and playing well . . . that scared a lot of guys before they even played us.

I knew when we beat Villanova that we were going to win the whole thing. With Raymond fouling out and me having to come in and play point guard, everybody on the bench was nervous. Every Tar Heel fan was nervous; the coaches were nervous. But I said, "Hey man, this is something I have to deal with. I'm ready. Let's do it."

I always dreamed of being in situations like that. I looked

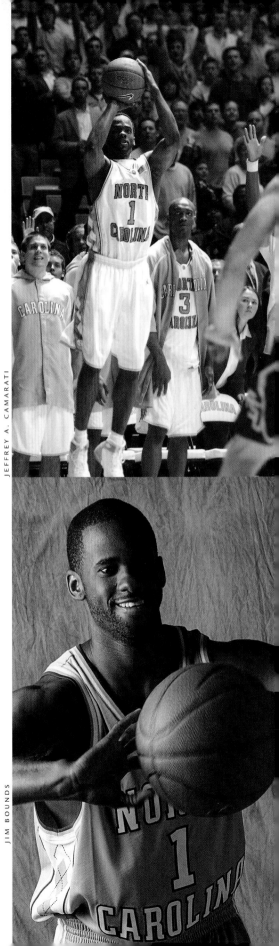

JEFFREY A. CAMARATI

at it as a huge opportunity to let people know that I can hit big shots. Coach Williams pulled me up in the huddle and said, "You've been in tougher situations than this. This is nothing." I looked at him and shook my head, "You're right." Then [with 28.9 seconds left and Carolina leading 64–62] I stepped up to the line and hit the two free throws.

Dealing with that kind of pressure is why I appreciate the 8 and 20 season so much. People look at me and say, "What are you talking about?" but if it wasn't for that, I wouldn't really know the game. I wouldn't be able to handle that pressure. I take positives from negative situations. Because we went 8 and 20 and I had to play point guard, it prepared me for playing in situations like the Villanova game.

We were the loosest team in St. Louis.

Sean's mom threw a birthday party for him, and we sang him a little song. However, we also were taking the criticism of our team very personally. At every meeting Coach Williams would read the papers to us, and guys were ticked off. We couldn't wait to prove those analysts wrong and go out and play like a team. We thank those analysts now because they helped us.

If we could make the Illinois guys take tough shots and guard them, I knew we were going to be victorious because they had nobody for Sean May. I was his biggest cheerleader. I was saying, "Get it to May, get it to May, get it to May." And he carried us on his back.

After the game Jawad, Jackie, and I were thanking God for all He's brought us through and telling each other that we loved each other. Coach

Williams came over, and we embraced him. We were praying and thanking God for blessing us with an opportunity to do something great. I always believed in God—that's how I changed my life around. I guess after the 8 and 20 season, after Coach Doherty resigned, I said, "There's got to be a better way." I had nothing else to live by because basketball, the love of my life, wasn't going well. I had to try something else to be happy, and going to church and doing Bible studies and staying strong in my faith was my getaway. Once you have all that in order, basketball is pretty easy.

I wouldn't trade being at Carolina for anything in the world.

North Carolina—the greatest came through here. You want to have that "NC" on your chest; you want to run out of that tunnel. It was always my dream, and where I come from, I never thought I'd get the opportunity. But I was blessed; this was the best experience of my life.

We're in a class with Jordan and Sam Perkins and guys like that. We're the dons again, so it's a great feeling. It's an honor, and they can never take that away from us.

Now my belt's got a new message: "Champs. National Champs."

Jawad Williams

Adapted from videotaped interviews

JEFFREY A. CAMARATI

We realized before the season that we could win it all.

Antawn Jamison, Makhtar Ndiaye—those guys talked to us last summer. That really helped us. It put everybody on the right track because they compared their 1998 team to ours and looked at why we weren't winning. We couldn't put a finger on it, and it all came down to us being a team. Then Makhtar called us the Chapel Hill Lakers. That stood out the most to me because it was true. We had all the talent in the world, but we didn't win anything. When we lost, we lost to better *teams*.

I decided to take everything my senior year one moment at a time—not one day at a time, one moment. Live for the moment and have fun with it. I enjoyed going to practice this year because I made myself have fun. The harder you work, the more fun you have.

J. Williams started 105 games in his Carolina career and averaged 14.5 points per game in the 2005 Final Four.

When you're a senior, a lot of guys feel it's their turn to shine. I tried to make my teammates realize that I wasn't going to be that type of player. Of course, everyone wants to go out there and be the leader—the leading scorer or whatever on a national championship team—but that wasn't my role. My role was to do whatever it took for my team to win because I was willing to do some of the little things that other guys wouldn't. I figured if I went out there and played hard every night and led by example, that would get my point across and everyone would follow.

I knew Marvin Williams was going to play a lot. When I came in as a freshman, people were talking about me competing with Jason [Capel] for a starting spot. I think it was the same thing with Marvin and me. I didn't care who got the starting job—I just wanted us to be successful. I wanted to take him under my wing, help him with little things and make sure he was happy. If he was happy, that made our team better.

I never cared who got the attention as long as we got the job done. If I just stayed under the radar, I could continue to do my thing and help lead my team. It all went back to my Bible—stay humble, and in due time you will be exalted.

Melvin Scott and Jackie Manuel are like my two brothers. Melvin is the one that plays all the time, and Jackie's the so-called quiet guy. Having those guys around makes life a lot easier. Melvin's always joking, keeping situations light, and Jackie—he's just there, for the most part. We enjoy each other's company. People don't know

> "I didn't care who got the starting job— I just wanted us to be successful."

that Melvin is actually a very spiritual person. But if you ever call his cell phone and listen to his voice mails, you always hear him quoting something from the Bible or some old guy with a lot of wisdom.

Some people may have been nervous when Melvin shot those free throws at the end of the Villanova game, but not me. I knew they were going to go in because when Melvin subbed into the game, he cracked jokes once again. It's a serious moment—everybody's tense—and Melvin runs by us, laughing on the court. They foul him; he's still laughing. I knew he was going to make the free throws because he was loose.

I definitely felt the level of respect the crowd showed me on Senior Day.

A lot of people behind the scenes here told me that I was unique because of the way I carried myself. There was nothing I did to carry myself higher than anyone else—it's just the way I am. I went out there and did everything quietly. I didn't want all the attention; I just wanted to get things done.

My dad, my mother, everybody in my family carries themselves that way. A lot of people misunderstand it as being arrogant. I'm just confident. I'm not going to say it out loud, but I am confident about the things I am capable of doing. I'm not going to back down from anybody; I'll look every man in his eye.

I didn't go to bed until 2:00 or 3:00 in the morning the night before the Duke game. I was up thinking the whole night. I was reading a magazine article about our experience and how far we've come. It almost brought tears to my eyes. I made Melvin read it. He said it almost brought tears to his eyes. So it was almost like, "We're here and we have a chance to do something very special, and we can leave our legacy behind if we go out here and get this W."

"It's amazing how much can be accomplished when no one cares who gets the credit." We wrote that up on the board in the locker room. That was our philosophy the whole year, and it made us successful.

KEVIN COX/WIRE IMAGE

JEFFREY A. CAMARATI

I knew when I felt we had something special. It was when we started getting the postseason awards and guys weren't satisfied. Actually, it wasn't the person who received the award that was upset. I received All-ACC third team, and I wasn't the one who was mad about it. I was actually happy because I had never received that before. Marvin Williams got mad for me. Raymond Felton got mad for me. Those guys voiced their opinion—they thought I should have gotten a better team than that. When my teammates were mad for me, that meant a lot. I wasn't satisfied when Jackie Manuel didn't get Defensive Player of the Year and Sean May wasn't ACC Player of the Year. That meant we were coming together as a team.

Guys were so anxious to play in the NCAA Tournament that we forgot about the ACC Tournament.

Once we got that loss to Georgia Tech, people started doubting us again. But the loss motivated us. Each loss was a wake-up call. It made us get back to the drawing board and get back to doing the fundamentals, because we beat ourselves. We didn't play defense well enough or we didn't make shots—it was always one of the two.

We worked even harder going into the NCAA Tournament. It was just a bigger stage, I believe. Guys were willing to try and go out there and leave their legacy. Everybody wanted to be part of something special.

I didn't play well the first two weekends of the tournament. I was sore [from a hip flexor injury], and I had a lot of tape and wraps on my leg that really restricted me. I couldn't get off the floor like I was used to; I couldn't push off the way I wanted to. I didn't say anything publicly about the injury because that's my personality—I'm not going to seek attention or help from anybody. Do it on my own—that's always been my mentality. I didn't need anybody else's excuses; I was just going to work through it. Finally, before the Final Four, I stopped babying myself. I talked to trainer Marc Davis and told him we had to take the tape off. He said, "But you're still hurting." I said, "Until my hip falls off, I'll be all right."

None of us had been to the Final Four before, but as a senior, I felt it was time for me to step up. Sean had been playing great, but for some reason against Michigan State I noticed that he wasn't

going to be himself for a half. I figured somebody had to step up. I was so confident that I even took terrible shots just because I had the confidence that they would fall. I wanted to go out there and establish myself early, regardless of whether that was taking good shots or bad shots.

I was really relaxed that last night [before the championship game]. I guess that came from visions I had of us winning. I knew it was only a matter of time before the clock ran out and we would be celebrating. I was trying to figure out what I was going to do when we did win. All the things I dreamed of—I did none of them. I remember running to the crowd, yelling at my mother. Then I remember trying to find my teammates, and they were off around half-court, so I just stood for a minute until Damion Grant came and got me.

Playing at Carolina was the greatest experience ever.

I am leaving here with ties that no one can ever break. I have a lot of people looking up to me right now. Hopefully I can continue to do the right thing and help these people achieve their goals.

The tough times were all worth it because now I am leaving as a national champion. A lot of guys can't say they have done that in their careers. A lot of guys will never be able to do that. It means a lot.

Marvin Williams

Adapted from videotaped interviews

BOB DONNAN

Being a Carolina basketball player is that pride you have—the tradition of winning, being a part of something so special.

That feeling of running out of the tunnel in the Smith Center is amazing. I remember the first time I did it; I was speechless. It's been a dream of mine to play at Carolina my whole life, so to run out of the tunnel every game is a special feeling.

A lot of people made a big deal out of the fact I never started a game in college, but to me it wasn't difficult at all. I just liked to win. Coach wanted me to do that, and that's what I did. It was what was best for our team. We had five great starters on the team that played well for us, so it was easy for me to be the sixth man. I was perfectly fine with that.

It kind of helped me, to be honest. I was more focused mentally when I came into the game, so that was better for me.

M. Williams averaged 11.3 points and 6.6 rebounds as a freshman. In 2005 he became Carolina's sixth ACC Rookie of the Year.

217

> "I'm pretty laid-back off the court, but I'm not that way when I play."

BOB DONNAN

It was tough at first to get settled to college ball. But the guys were great. I would walk into practice every day, and if I needed anything, I could talk to Jawad or Sean. They were big-time for me. I wish everybody had a chance to meet Jawad because he's a good person. He cares about people. He's a senior so he had a lot to tell me, a lot to teach me, and I listened to him. It was good for me.

Jawad told me to keep working hard. He said there were going to be ups and downs my whole career. Some games I'd have good games; some games I wouldn't. He said to stay tough and keep working hard, and good things will turn out.

I worked as hard as I could to help Jawad and Sean in practice. In games, they were so important for us to have on the floor, so when they got tired or they got in foul trouble, I had to come in and fill those shoes, which was tough. I tried to do the best I could.

I'm pretty laid-back off the court, but I'm not that way when I play. Everybody tells me that. I haven't figured it out yet. I think it's the passion I have for the game. I want to win so badly that I'm pretty intense. It's a good thing.

My mom got to see me play about four or five times this year.

My mother is my hero. She took care of my two brothers and me by herself our whole lives. She's so special to us. I can't even put it into words what she means to me.

I did get to surprise her with a visit back in the fall when Coach gave us a weekend off. I told my mom I couldn't make it home because a recruit had come in. I called my uncle, and he picked me up at the airport around 11:00 at night—so I got home about 12:30 in the morning. I walked into the house and was talking to my mom on my cell phone, and she asked, "Why are you up so late? It's 3:30 over there." I was digging in the refrigerator and the cabinets, still talking to her. Finally I opened her door. It was dark in there, so she thought it was my little brother (he's pretty tall, too). I finally turned on the lights, and she stared at me for a second and jumped up and started screaming. That was pretty funny.

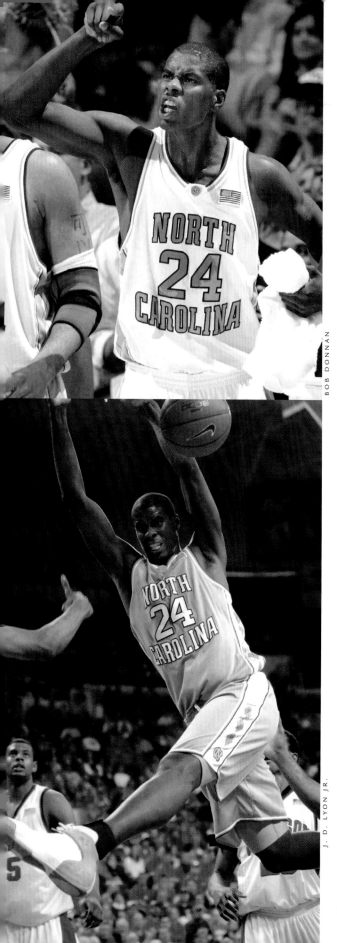

BOB DONNAN

J. D. LYON JR.

We started the year by losing to Santa Clara, and I didn't know what to think.

That was my first college basketball game, so I was pretty overwhelmed. We were ranked No. 1 in the country, and nobody expected that loss. That was tough on us, but I really feel that was what we needed. I don't think we would have been the same team without losing that game.

We felt we were good, but we weren't as good as everybody said. We knew we had to get better, and Coach Williams did a good job of getting us better.

The practices in Maui were awful. Those were probably the toughest practices all year; everybody had to work hard. But I mean it was tough for *me*. I'm a freshman, and I hadn't experienced anything like that before. But I got through it.

The biggest adjustments I had to make to college ball were on defense because everybody is so quick and strong. Offensively, Coach Williams kept faith in me. The coaches screamed at me every day to shoot the ball because I wasn't shooting enough. Coach Holladay would tell me to shoot, and Coach Williams would tell me to shoot. They had a lot of confidence in me.

I did have a couple of dunks that were pretty memorable. My favorites were the ones at Florida State, in the NCAA first round against Oakland, and in the win over NC State here in the Smith Center. During the one at FSU, I knew that [Alexander Johnson] was coming, but I didn't know that he was going to continue to run. I took one dribble and dunked, and he was there. I surprised myself.

Beating Duke at home was fun. Ray missed a free throw [in the last 20 seconds of the game], and everybody was fighting for the ball. I grabbed it and threw it in and got fouled. You have to give Ray the credit. He could have been upset after missing the free

throw and given up, but he kept fighting, and Sean was fighting. The ball popped out, and I grabbed it. After the game everything was wild. I saw my brothers out there on the court, so I was smiling. It was probably the biggest moment of my life, as far as sports goes.

Coach gave us a pledge to sign before the Final Four.

That pledge meant a lot. You told your teammates you weren't going to let them down for the next seven days. Everybody took that personally, and everybody worked hard to keep that promise.

All the talk at the Final Four about us not being a team was very upsetting to everybody. People said Carolina couldn't play defense, Carolina wasn't a team; we weren't tough enough. Well, we proved to everybody we were as good a team as anybody else. The best team won. Illinois is a great team—but we do have some guys that can play basketball.

In the championship game I got a tip-in with a minute and a half left to give us the lead, and it turned out to be the winning basket. Rashad was trying to make a play, and one of the defenders got a block on his shot. The ball was up in the air, and I went after it as hard as I could. I knew Rashad was going to try to score—you could see it in his eyes. So I went to the block on the reverse side and was able to tip it in.

When the buzzer sounded, I was so happy that I dropped to my knees and prayed. I thanked God for that experience, for us to win that game. What I will remember most about this year are the guys and the experiences we had. We had some tough times, and we had some good times. You'll never forget the teammates you did that with. It was a long journey, but we all stuck together and pulled it out.

A Tribute to
Burgess McSwain

About an hour after Carolina defeated Michigan State in the Final Four, the Tar Heel locker room was relatively quiet.

Most of the players were in the shower or had trekked to the team bus in a loading area of the Edward Jones Dome. Almost all of the media were gone, too, with only a lone television crew and a sportswriter talking casually to Marvin Williams in a corner.

A few feet away, senior Melvin Scott silently wrote on a dry-erase board: "1 More Win for Ms. Burgess, R.I.P."

Not many people noticed, and that's probably the way Burgess McSwain would have wanted it. An academic advisor to the Tar Heel men's basketball program, McSwain worked with the squad for more than two decades without allowing athletic department officials to publish her photo in the team's media guide.

McSwain and her father at a game (opposite); McSwain tutoring Scott (above).

She finally relented before the 2003–04 season but did not get a chance to do so the following year. McSwain died on July 9, 2004, at the age of 60, as a result of complications from surgery. She had been battling cancer for several years.

McSwain was not just a tutor who pulled all-nighters to help players prepare for exams after late road games; she also was a surrogate mother to several generations of Tar Heel players living away from home for the first time.

"What Melvin wrote on the board meant a lot because guys still had her in the back of their minds," said Jawad Williams. "I remember before the Illinois game, there were two seats open in the pregame meeting. There was one on the end and one in the middle, right in front of the board. No one was sitting in the middle, so I think the team left it open for me. For some strange reason, I thought, 'I'm going to leave that open; that's where Burgess would sit if she came into this room right now.' She was in the back of our minds. She really watched over us. We owe her a lot."

Sean May told a similar story. "We all had our own reason for winning it—for Coach, for ourselves, for our seniors—but somebody wrote on the board 'Let's get it done for Burgess,' and that really hit home. I sat there and stared at that for a couple minutes. Sometimes when someone's gone, you don't realize how much you miss them."

Jackie Manuel added, "We all wished she could have been in St. Louis, to see that smile on her faces. She was one of those people this national championship was won for."

Few individuals were privy to more of Carolina basketball's behind-the-scenes stories than McSwain, but Carolina players knew that their secrets were safe with her. McSwain was an intensely private person, which helps to explain why she was so beloved by Tar Heels from Phil Ford to Rashad McCants. Carolina basketball players are celebrities in Chapel Hill, and they often come to value people who treat them as individuals rather than simply athletes.

JEFFREY A. CAMARATI

Burgess McSwain
1944–2004

"She was my mom away from home," Scott said of McSwain after winning the national title. "She was the first person I learned to trust here. When basketball was so frustrating that we didn't even want to go to practice, we'd just go to her house. Sometimes we didn't even study; she'd just talk to us and let us know that we would be fine and that there would be a brighter day. That love, you know—that's the love you only get from home."

Carolina had the highest graduation rate among the Sweet 16 teams in the NCAA Tournament. That statistic, and the program's long-standing and impressive graduation rate, are results of McSwain's efforts.

Manuel, J. Williams, Everett, and Scott with Chancellor James Moeser.

"Melvin will be the first one in his family to graduate from college, and she's the main reason why," May said. "She made sure we were on track; she made sure we went to class; she made sure we did the things that we were supposed to do. She's someone I will never forget."

Scott, Manuel, and Jawad Williams, having endured the most arduous of freshman seasons in 2001–02 and a tumultuous coaching change a year later, all had particularly strong bonds with McSwain.

"Without her, I wouldn't be here," Williams said. "She kept us together. She knew our entire life. She didn't care who scored the most points, who played the most minutes. She wanted us to graduate. That was her main thing."

Like many, Burgess McSwain loved to root for the Tar Heels. You have to assume that, somewhere, she was watching her boys win the national championship, cheering as loudly as anyone. But she may have been happier when Manuel, Scott, and Jawad Williams graduated from Carolina on May 15, 2005. It's a shame she wasn't there to see it in person.

—MATT BOWERS

JEFFREY A. CAMARATI

Front row (l-r): Manager Russ Lauten, Strength and Conditioning Coordinator Jonas Sahratian, Administrative Assistant and Assistant Strength & Conditioning Coordinator Jerod Haase, Assistant Coach Steve Robinson, Assistant Coach Joe Holladay, Raymond Felton, Jackie Manuel, Jawad Williams, Melvin Scott, C. J. Hooker, Rashad McCants, Head Coach Roy Williams, Assistant Coach C. B. McGrath, Trainer Marc Davis, Video Coordinator Eric Hoots, Head Manager David Hoots

Back row (l-r): Manager Kathryn Howlett, Manager Zane Hendrix, Brooks Foster, Wes Miller, Charlie Everett, Reyshawn Terry, Byron Sanders, Damion Grant, Sean May, Marvin Williams, David Noel, Quentin Thomas, Jesse Holley, Manager Preston Puckett, Manager Bradley Vanhoy

2004–05 University of North Carolina Men's Basketball Roster

No.	Player	Yr.	Pos.	Ht.	Wt.	Hometown	High School
0	Jesse Holley	So.	G	6-3	190	Roselle, NJ	Abraham Clark
1	Melvin Scott	Sr.	G	6-2	190	Baltimore, MD	Southern
2	Raymond Felton	Jr.	G	6-1	198	Latta, SC	Latta
3	Reyshawn Terry	So.	F	6-8	214	Winston-Salem, NC	R. J. Reynolds
4	Brooks Foster	Fr.	G	6-2	190	Boiling Springs, SC	Boiling Springs
5	Jackie Manuel	Sr.	G/F	6-5	192	West Palm Beach, FL	Cardinal Newman
11	Quentin Thomas	Fr.	G	6-3	185	Oakland, CA	Oakland Technical Senior
15	Charlie Everett	Sr.	F	6-3	210	Charlotte, NC	South Mecklenburg
21	Jawad Williams	Sr.	F	6-9	220	Cleveland, OH	St. Edwards
22	Wes Miller	So.	G	5-11	185	Charlotte, NC	New Hampton Prep (NH)
24	Marvin Williams	Fr.	F	6-9	230	Bremerton, WA	Bremerton
25	Damion Grant	Jr.	C	6-11	260	Portland, Jamaica	Brewster Academy (NH)
32	Rashad McCants	Jr.	F/G	6-4	207	Asheville, NC	New Hampton Prep (NH)
34	David Noel	Jr.	F	6-6	230	Durham, NC	Southern Durham
35	C. J. Hooker	Sr.	F	6-2	188	Palmer, AK	Palmer
41	Byron Sanders	Jr.	F	6-9	230	Gulfport, MS	Harrison Central
42	Sean May	Jr.	F/C	6-9	260	Bloomington, IN	Bloomington North

Head Coach: Roy Williams
Assistant Coaches: Joe Holladay, Steve Robinson, C. B. McGrath
Administrative Assistant and Assistant Strength and Conditioning Coordinator: Jerod Haase
Strength and Conditioning Coordinator: Jonas Sahratian
Trainer: Marc Davis
Video Coordinator: Eric Hoots

2004–05 Season Record

33–4, 14–2 ACC

November

19	vs. Santa Clara (Oakland)	L	66–77	Minus Felton, UNC shoots 36%; SC scores 48 in second half
22	vs. BYU (Maui)	W	86–50	UNC races to 31–6 lead, 48–18 at halftime; forces 27 turnovers
23	vs. Tennessee (Maui)	W	94–81	McCants and J. Williams combine on 18 of 26 FGs, 48 points
24	vs. Iowa (Maui)	W	106–92	Felton tournament MVP with 13 points, 9 assists, 4 steals; McCants 22 points
28	USC	W	97–65	UNC doubles Trojan score at half (56–28); shoots 57% FG for game

December

1	at Indiana	W	70–63	Five 3FGs from McCants help compensate for 23 UNC turnovers
4	Kentucky	W	91–78	May 19 rebounds, McCants 28 points as UNC ends four-game losing streak to UK
12	Loyola	W	109–60	Six Tar Heels in double figures; largest win margin of year (49 points)
19	at Virginia Tech	W	85–51	UNC shoots 65.5% FG; ends first half on 22–7 run in ACC opener
21	Vermont	W	93–65	May scores 20, J. Williams limits VT star Coppenrath to 13 points
28	UNC Wilmington	W	96–75	UNC opens with 13–0 run; J. Williams nets 25, Felton 10 assists
30	Cleveland State	W	107–64	May (16 points) leads six Tar Heels in double figures; UNC forces 31 turnovers

January

2	William & Mary	W	105–66	May 24 points, Felton 12 assists; Carolina scores 50+ in both halves
8	Maryland	W	109–75	23–5 run in first half; most points ever by UNC vs. Terps; seven Tar Heels in double figures
12	Georgia Tech	W	91–69	McCants 4 blocks; Tech shoots 37% FG and commits 19 turnovers
15	at Wake Forest	L	82–95	Paul 26 points, 8 assists; McCants 19 points in only 20 minutes
19	at Clemson	W	77–58	Tied at 27 at half; McCants scores 17 of game-high 23 in second half
22	Miami	W	87–67	May 17 points and 15 rebounds; Miami shoots 29% FG in first half
29	at Virginia	W	110–76	UNC scores 62 in first half; J. Williams 23 points, M. Williams 10 rebounds

February

3	NC State	W	95–71	M. Williams three 3FGs, first 20-point game; UNC shoots 60% FG, NC State 39%
6	at Florida State	W	81–60	25–6 UNC run in second half after FSU closes to within 49–48
9	at Duke	L	70–71	May 23 points, 18 rebounds; UNC 23 turnovers; Duke 17 steals
13	at Connecticut	W	77–70	J. Williams hits three 3FGs; May 16 points, 13 rebounds
16	Virginia	W	85–61	McCants (23 points) hits 9 of 12 FG; May adds 16 rebounds
19	Clemson	W	88–56	Defense forces 27 turnovers, limits Tigers to 33% FG; Felton 9 assists
22	at NC State	W	81–71	Scott hits four 3FGs; Felton 21 points, 7 rebounds, 0 turnovers
27	at Maryland	W	85–83	Felton lay-up with 19 seconds remaining; May blocks last-second Maryland shot

March

| 3 | Florida State | W | 91–76 | May 32 points, 12 rebounds; Felton 10 assists; Noel 8 assists |
| 6 | Duke | W | 75–73 | May 26 points, 24 rebounds; UNC wins ACC outright first time since 1993; M. Williams three-point play provides winning margin |

ACC Tournament (Washington, D.C.)

| 11 | vs. Clemson | W | 88–81 | Felton 29 points; McCants 13 points in return from illness |
| 12 | vs. Georgia Tech | L | 75–78 | UNC shoots season-low 36.1% FG; Will Bynum nets 35 for GT |

NCAA First and Second Rounds (Charlotte, NC)

| 18 | vs. Oakland | W | 96–68 | UNC shoots 73.3% FG; M. Williams 20 points; May 19 points |
| 20 | vs. Iowa State | W | 92–65 | May and M. Williams combine for 44 points, 32 rebounds |

NCAA Syracuse Regional (Syracuse, NY)

| 25 | vs. Villanova | W | 67–66 | McCants 15 points in second half; Scott holds off Wildcats with free throws |
| 27 | vs. Wisconsin | W | 88–82 | MVP May dominates with 29 points, 12 rebounds; late 3FG and block from McCants |

April

NCAA Final Four (St. Louis, MO)

| 2 | vs. Michigan State | W | 87–71 | UNC down 38–33 at halftime; May 22 points; J. Williams 20 points |
| 4 | vs. Illinois | W | 75–70 | MVP May 26 points, 10 rebounds; Felton 17 points, 7 assists, last-minute steal; M. Williams tips in winner with 1:27 remaining |

Postseason Notes

In 2004–05 Carolina . . .

- made its eighth appearance in the NCAA championship game.
- made its 21st appearance in the NCAA Elite Eight.
- made its NCAA-record 16th appearance in the Final Four.
- on average outscored NCAA Tournament opponents 84.2 to 70.3, outshot them 51.4 to 39.3 percent, and outrebounded them 41.5 to 35.3.
- averaged 88 points per game and became the third team to lead the nation in scoring offense and win the NCAA title (joining Loyola of Chicago, 1963, and Ohio State, 1960).
- beat No. 1 ranked Illinois in the first meeting between the AP's first- and second-ranked teams in the NCAA title game since 1975.
- posted an ACC record of 14–2. It marked the 30th time in 52 years that UNC has won 10 or more conference games.
- won the regular-season ACC title for the 24th time overall and 15th time outright. It marked the first time the Tar Heels improved from fifth to first place in the ACC in a single season.
- led the ACC in scoring (88 points per game), scoring margin (+17.8 points per game), field goal percentage (49.9), three-point field goal percentage (40.3), rebounding margin (+7.5), and assists (19.1 per game).
- went 33–4 overall, the second-highest win total in school history (behind the 1992–93 record of 34–4).
- won 18 consecutive games at the Smith Center, equaling the third-longest streak in the building's history.
- beat teams at home by an average of 26.5 points per game.
- shot 50 percent or better from the floor in 41 of 74 halves of play.
- went 27–1 when scoring more than 80 points in a game.
- went 26–0 when leading at halftime.
- went 20–0 when shooting 50 percent or better from the floor, 18–2 when holding opponents to less than 40 percent shooting, and 28–1 when having a rebounding advantage.
- made 277 three-pointers, the second most in school history.
- had 362 steals, a single-season school record.

Roy Williams . . .

- is the third coach to lead two different teams to the NCAA championship game (Kansas in 1991 and 2003; UNC in 2005).
- has five Final Four appearances, the sixth most for a coach in NCAA history (behind John Wooden, Dean Smith, Mike Krzyewski, Denny Crum, and Adolph Rupp).
- has 16 straight NCAA appearances, the second-longest active streak and the third-longest all-time. He has won at least one game in each tournament. (Dean Smith holds the record with at least one win in 17 consecutive NCAA Tournaments, 1981–97.)
- has 41 all-time NCAA Tournament wins, fourth among active coaches and seventh all-time.

The Players

- Raymond Felton led the ACC in assists for the second year in a row. He joins Ed Cota and Phil Ford as the only Tar Heels to lead the league in assists in consecutive seasons.
- Felton finished his career with 698 assists, the fourth-highest total in UNC history behind Ed Cota (1,030), Kenny Smith (768), and Phil Ford (753). Only Cota had more assists in a three-year career.
- Jackie Manuel is the first Tar Heel to be named to the All-ACC defensive team more than once. As a senior he was named Carolina's defensive player of the game 14 times.
- Sean May and his father, Scott (Indiana), are the third father-son duo to win an NCAA title, joining Henry (UCLA) and Mike Bibby (Arizona) and Marques and Kris Johnson (UCLA).
- May hit 10 of 11 shots (90.9 percent) against Illinois, the second-best shooting performance in NCAA championship game history.
- May had 397 rebounds in 2005, breaking Antawn Jamison's school record.
- May averaged 15.8 points and 10 rebounds in his 77-game college career. He is one of only seven Tar Heels to average a career double-double and the first to do so since 1972. He posted double-doubles in 13 of his last 15 games.

- May set records for most rebounds by a Tar Heel against Duke and most rebounds in the Smith Center (24).
- Rashad McCants scored 1,721 points in his three-year career, the seventh-highest total among UNC players who stayed three seasons and the 14th-highest in school history.
- McCants made 221 three-point field goals, tying him for second all-time at UNC (with Donald Williams; Shammond Williams holds the record with 233).
- Melvin Scott made 183 three-point baskets, the seventh-best total in UNC history.
- Marvin Williams shot 84.7 percent from the free throw line, the highest percentage of any freshman and the highest percentage of any forward or center in the conference in 2004–05.
- M. Williams is second all-time at Carolina in free throw percentage (.847) among players with at least 100 made free throws (behind Shammond Williams, .849).

Awards and Honors

Raymond Felton

- Bob Cousy Collegiate Point Guard of the Year
- NCAA Final Four All-Tournament Team
- Third-team All-America (Associated Press)
- Honorable Mention All-America (*Sports Illustrated*)
- First-team All-ACC
- All-ACC Tournament Team
- Honorable Mention ACC All-Defensive Team
- All-Mid-Atlantic Region (*Basketball Times*)
- ACC Player of the Week (February 28, 2005)
- Maui Invitational MVP

Sean May

- NCAA Final Four MVP
- NCAA Tournament Syracuse Regional MVP
- NCAA Tournament All-Syracuse Regional Team
- First-team All-America (ESPN.com and Rupp)
- Consensus Second-team All-America
- Second-team All-America (Associated Press, *Sports Illustrated,* USBWA, *Sporting News,* and *Basketball Times*)
- First-team All-ACC
- Wooden Award finalist
- 2004 USA Basketball Co-Player of the Year (with Chris Paul of Wake Forest)
- ACC Player of the Week (March 7, 2005)

Jackie Manuel

- ACC All-Defensive Team (media and coaches)
- Third in voting for ACC Defensive Player of the Year

Rashad McCants

- NCAA Final Four All-Tournament Team
- NCAA Tournament All-Syracuse Regional Team
- Third-team All-America (NABC)
- Third-team All-ACC
- All-Mid-Atlantic Region (*Basketball Times*)
- Wooden Award finalist
- Maui Invitational All-Tournament Team
- National Player of the Week (*Sporting News,* November 22–27, 2004)

Jawad Williams

- Third-team All-ACC
- All-Support Team (Dick Vitale)

Marvin Williams

- ACC Rookie of the Year
- ACC All-Freshman Team (unanimous selection)
- Honorable Mention All-ACC
- First-team All-Freshman (*Basketball Times*)
- ACC Rookie of the Week (November 29 and December 20, 2004; January 31, February 7, and March 7, 2005)